T0346475

"For many of us, the biggest battles we fight are those in our own minds. In his new book, *Mind Shift*, Erwin McManus leads readers to lasting change by helping them shift how they think. As a result of decades of research and personal reflection, McManus writes with raw transparency and uses life-altering instruction to coach readers toward a fuller life. This book is for anyone who knows they can do more and are tired of settling for less."

—Craig Groeschel, pastor of Life.Church, bestselling author of *Winning the War in Your Mind*

"Erwin McManus's wisdom has been instrumental in shaping my life over the last fifteen years. With decades of experience building up communities, companies, and leaders across industries, McManus inspires us to move from apathy to action. *Mind Shift* is the book for those called to build the things the world needs most."

—Brad Damphousse, co-founder of GoFundMe and founder of AutoGive

MIND SHIFT

MIND SHIFT

It Doesn't Take a Genius
to Think Like One

ERWIN RAPHAEL McMANUS

CONVERGENT
NEW YORK

Published in the United States by Convergent Books,
an imprint of Random House, a division of
Penguin Random House LLC, New York.

CONVERGENT BOOKS is a registered trademark
and the Convergent colophon is a trademark of
Penguin Random House LLC.

LIBRARY OF CONGRESS CATALOGING-IN-PUBLICATION DATA
Names: McManus, Erwin Raphael, author.
Title: Mind shift / Erwin Raphael McManus.
Description: First edition. | New York, NY: Convergent Books, 2023
Identifiers: LCCN 2023020874 (print) | LCCN 2023020875 (ebook) |
ISBN 9780593137413 (hardcover) | ISBN 9780593137420 (ebook)
Subjects: LCSH: Motivation (Psychology) | Success. | Decision making.
Classification: LCC BF503 .M454 2023 (print) | LCC BF503 (ebook) |
DDC 158.1—dc23/eng/20230620
LC record available at https://lccn.loc.gov/2023020874
LC ebook record available at https://lccn.loc.gov/2023020875

Printed in Canada

convergentbooks.com

2 4 6 8 9 7 5 3

Book design by Alexis Capitini

To Jesus
who created in me a Mind Shift
that transformed my life from the inside out.
You changed my heart,
changed my mind,
and changed my life.

CONTENTS

Writing *Mind Shift* is the culmination of a personal journey that has resulted in seismic shifts in my own life.

This book is in many ways a significant pivot moving my private work into my public life.

I have had the privilege of advising and coaching and serving as a personal think tank for entrepreneurs and creators for decades.

I have served them but they have equally served me.

They are the best at what they do and they have brought the best out of me.

They have convinced me of the value of going public and of the importance of taking my work and insights to a broader audience.

They opened new doors and new worlds believing in the contribution I could make.

Frankly, I didn't even know what it meant when I was first introduced as a polymath.

If it is true that you become the sum total of the people in your life, then I am set for life.

I would like to dedicate this book to the brothers who have journeyed with me and encouraged me to launch my Mastermind for elite-level thinkers and leaders.

You guys always have my back. We are bound by sweat and blood and tears.

My favorite films all have a common theme. *The Seven Samurai, The Magnificent Seven, The Dirty Dozen, Band of Brothers, Braveheart.* They are all stories about men who become brothers and come together to achieve the impossible.

In the dog-eat-dog world of business, these men are my band of brothers:

Jon Gordon	David Maura
Joel Marion	Jacob Koo
Paulo Lima	Kent Clothier
Ed Mylett	Kevin Loo
Lewis Howes	Aaron Bartz
Edwin Arroyave	Todd Abrams
Sasha Leahovcenco	Aaron McManus

With you heart and soul.

The intention of this book
is to
destroy your internal limitations.

—Erwin Raphael McManus

MIND SHIFT

Change Your Mind

"Some people are simply structured for failure." I will never forget the moment I heard those words as I was driving through downtown Dallas listening to sports radio. Though the host was trying to explain what had happened the day before in the boxing world, the words have haunted me ever since.

Eight months earlier, Buster Douglas had erupted onto the boxing scene by knocking out the undefeated world heavyweight champion Mike Tyson. Like Muhammad Ali, Joe Frazier, and George Foreman before him, Tyson was a heavyweight who defined boxing for a generation. For fans of the sport, he represented the most devastating, ferocious, and terrifying fighter who ever walked into a ring. Tyson didn't simply defeat his opponents; he destroyed them. Only two years earlier, he had beaten then champion Michael Spinks by knocking him out in the first round. Tyson's last opponent before Douglas had made it only ninety-one seconds before a vicious left hook dropped him to the mat.

The fight between Douglas and Tyson took place in Tokyo, Japan, with Tyson a 42-to-1 favorite not only to defeat Buster Douglas but to render him unconscious. The outcome of this contest seemed inevitable. Except, of course, no one told Buster Douglas that it was impossible for him to win. After ten rounds of holding his own against the most dangerous man in the world, Douglas did the unthinkable. He knocked Mike Tyson out and walked away with three world heavyweight belts.

Now, eight months later, Douglas was defending his title for the first time against Evander Holyfield. He went into that fight overweight and out of shape, weighing in fifteen pounds heavier than when he faced Mike Tyson. In the ring, he was slow and sluggish, and he looked nothing like the champion who had defeated Tyson. For two rounds, Holyfield completely dominated Douglas. Then in the third, Douglas threw a telegraphed uppercut that was so out of control he lost his balance. That's when Holyfield threw the counterpunch that knocked him out.

Douglas's reign as the greatest heavyweight boxer in the world ended with him flat on his back, motionless, disoriented, and defeated. He retired after that fight and soon ballooned to nearly four hundred pounds, nearly dying from a diabetic coma.

The tragedy of this story is not that Buster Douglas lost his belt in the very first defense of his title. Neither is it that he lost to a superior fighter who would now reign as champion himself. The tragedy is that he didn't even try. The theme of the fight was "The Moment Of Truth!" It could not have been more accurate. We do not know the details of Buster's preparation—or lack of it. I remember hearing stories that he was seen at McDonald's the day of the fight. And while that nuance might be apocryphal, what is undeniable is what happened in the ring. Success turned out to be the anomaly for Douglas; sadly, it was not his internal structure.

Which brings us back to that boxing expert, who in one brief moment opened Pandora's box. *Some people are simply structured for failure.* The idea began to haunt me. Can a human being really be structured for failure? More personally, am *I* structured for failure? Have I consciously or unconsciously embraced mental frameworks that essentially destine me to fail? Can these frameworks be so subtle that they cause me to live beneath my full capacity or even lead to self-sabotage?

The answer is an ominous yes.

But I am an eternal optimist, so instead this epiphany flooded into my brain like morning sunlight. If my mind can be structured for failure, then it can also be structured for success.

This is the premise of every chapter in this book. Within all of us, there are mental structures that not only shape our thinking but shape *us*. If you believe you are incapable of learning another language, you likely will be bad at languages. If you believe people never change, you will never change. If you believe you cannot succeed, you will fail. Researchers have even found that the level of physical pain you can endure is mostly in your head. These mental constructs have more to do with our failure and success than any external factor. It doesn't matter who your opponent is when you step into the ring. If you are structured for failure, a lesser foe will drop you to the mat.

Fortunately this works the other way as well. Your mental structures can unlock untapped potential and unleash unimaginable capability. I have witnessed this many times. Your body can heal from a traumatic injury when your mental fortitude pushes you through the pain of therapy. You can overcome setbacks that would be insurmountable for others when you believe that you are unstoppable. You will surpass expectations and confound your doubters when you are convinced that hard work is more important than talent. There is an ancient proverb that tells us that you become your thoughts. Your thoughts are the road map to your future. If you transform your thinking, you will transform your life.

I've spent my life trying to change people's minds. In a way, it's ironic. Everyone knows that you can't change anyone's mind except your own. But I've given my life to the mission of helping others become the best version of themselves. I love watching people grow, change, and achieve what they previously thought was impossible, and I've done this in dramatically varied contexts.

I've spent four decades working as a social entrepreneur, community developer, and faith leader. For my first ten years out of college, I invested in people who faced extreme poverty and lacked formal education—many of whom were in street gangs and violent drug cartels. For another decade I worked as a futurist for universities and global organizations, designing strategies and degree programs that moved the institutions toward relevance. During this time, I traveled globally, consulting with thousands of leaders and speaking to millions as an expert on transformation and optimal performance—both personally and organizationally. For the last decade, I have dedicated a significant part of my life to coaching and advising high-capacity entrepreneurs.

In the midst of all that, I founded a church in Los Angeles called Mosaic. Our principal campus sits on Hollywood Boulevard, with additional locations and houses across the world. Our community's average age is twenty-six and it is populated by what the media has described as the highest concentration of industry artists in the world. Every week approximately twenty thousand people access messages focused on their spiritual well-being and personal transformation.

Identifying, developing, and optimizing talent has been the unifying theme in all of my work. One thing that's become clear to me is that really good people can make really bad decisions. The kind person forfeiting their dreams while waiting on friends and loved ones to affirm their new direction. The caring leader surrendering the future of her organization in an effort to keep everyone on board. The world-class athlete ignoring how his hyperfocus is crippling his relationships and stealing his happiness. The highly successful entrepreneur trying to fix his marriage as if it were a business. The person who has always performed for the approval of others discovering that they lack the resilience required to master the skills of their craft.

Though we may sense that we have a recurring problem, we are blind to the patterns of thought and behavior that create the same problem over and over again. Knowing how to help people break through their self-limiting beliefs and unlock latent potential has been the key to my personal success and the critical component in helping others achieve. That work has been as monumental as helping them find their life's great ambition, or as simple as reminding them that when they walk into a room, they belong there.

I turn sixty-four years old as I write this book. Maybe it's a function of my age, but the number one question I get when I travel the world is this: What would you tell your twenty-five-year-old self?

For the longest time, the question irritated me. Is that really the only thing people want to know? However, in retrospect, it's a great question. What people are actually asking is: What can you see now that you couldn't see then? What do you see now that we need to see? The fact that this is the one thing people seem desperate to know tells me that we all long to maximize the one life we have, and most of us don't feel confident that we know how to do that.

Growing older, by itself, is no great accomplishment. Mostly it means I've avoided death so far. (That, by the way, has been no small feat. I have been close to death many times—facing down both gunmen ready to shoot and stage four cancer that had already metastasized—but that's not the point of this book.) However, I've learned that, unfortunately, most of us not only avoid near-death experiences, we avoid near-life experiences as well. We *almost* risk for love. We *almost* pursue our dreams. We *almost* overcome our fears. We *almost* live the life we long for. We *almost* make the decision that would have changed everything. And then we get to the end of our lives and realize that we were so close. We were always just one choice away.

Life is an unpredictable and beautiful journey filled with both adventure and danger. That is, of course, if you choose life rather than existence. Life doesn't just *happen*. If your life is happening by accident, you are only existing. If you are living beneath your potential, you are only existing. If you've surrendered your uniqueness for acceptance, you are only existing. If you are living for pleasure and profit rather than love and purpose, you are only existing.

For most of us, the tension is not between good choices and bad choices. The real battle is between the *easy good* and the *hard best*. Did you choose the wrong major? Did you choose the wrong career? The wrong partner? The wrong city? The wrong dream? Did you settle? It's so easy to get it all wrong.

It's as though there is a gravitational pull toward mediocrity. The more determined you are to maximize your life, the more challenges you will face. The more you are unwilling to be satisfied with the status quo, the more you will find yourself facing resistance. It's tempting to choose the easy road, to settle for mere existence. But the obstacles and challenges and crises you face are not interruptions or detours on the path of life. They are the very context for life itself.

That's why I wrote this book. Mental health, mental clarity, mental toughness, and mental agility all have one thing in common: The journey begins in our minds. This is where the battle is fought—and where the battle is won. Every time you want to elevate your level of execution, performance, or effectiveness, it will require a mind shift. For anything to change, the first thing that must change is your mind. I've come to realize after forty years of working with people who were both desperate and determined to change their lives that my real occupation is a mind architect. Over the next chapters, if you'll allow me, I will guide you on a journey to redesign your inner world and create the mental architecture for success.

I have condensed six decades of personal experience and research into twelve mental structures that will set you free to be fully alive. Some of them involve our work and the dreams we're chasing for our careers. Others involve our relationships, the hopes and fears that drive our everyday decisions. Each mind shift will help you identify and remove the internal structures of failure, while helping you build the internal framework for success.

What I hope to convince you of through these mind shifts is that you don't need to know *what* to see nearly as much as you need to know *how* to see. When we only perceive the face value, short-term benefit, or immediate gratification of a choice, we allow self-limiting structures to be established in our minds. The twelve mind shifts will give you the eyes to see beyond the present opportunity to its future implications. You don't have to see the future to create it. You only need to see the patterns that create that future. If you've been dreaming about a life that seems elusive and impossible, I hope to change your mind. Once these mental constructs are yours, you will never see the world the same way again.

There's a shift happening inside of you. Can you feel it? Your imagination is not a toy, it is a tool. The future is waiting for those with the courage to create it. If you are tired of illusions and are ready to turn dreams into reality, if you are tired of existing and are ready to live, then it is time for a mind shift. You may not be able to see it yet, but the change is coming. Transform your thinking. Transform your life.

If you could create a social experiment to test the limits of mental health, mental clarity, mental toughness, and mental agility, it would look a lot like *The Walking Dead*, the TV series created by Frank Darabont where a virus changes the landscape of human existence. For eleven seasons, I faithfully followed the life of Rick Grimes, a sheriff who awakes in a hospital bed after the world has been overtaken by zombies. The entire story seems to ask one simple question: Can a person remain good when the entire world goes bad?

At first, the audience thinks the danger to humanity's survival is the "walkers," as they are called. Soon they realize that the real danger is the living. Or perhaps that's an overstatement. The survivors on the show are not living at all. They are consumed by fear, hate, greed, and power, and driven to unspeakable violence. They are worse than the dead. They are not the walking dead, they are the living dead.

Flash forward to the final episode of this cult classic. In the closing moments of the show, the characters we've come to know and love—at least the ones who have survived—begin to chant a final proclamation. All season, I had wondered what the final line in the show would be. One by one, the characters all begin to say the same thing—at first individually, then in unison. The line paralyzed me. It took my breath away.

"We are the ones who live!"

That's who we are.
That's who I am.
That's who you are.
Existing isn't enough.
Surviving isn't enough.
This is why we fight.
We rise above the fray.
We set the new standard.
We reclaim our humanity.
We create the future.
We are the unstoppable.
We are the ones who tell the story.
We are the ones who live.

It's All About People

I'm beginning here because if you miss this one, nothing else in the following chapters will matter.

The longer you live, the more you come to realize that it is inevitable that you will lose things. You will lose hundreds of socks in the dryer—never both, only one of each pair. You will probably lose your wallet, and with it, your driver's license, credit cards, and the cash you were carrying for an emergency. If you are anything like me, you will lose your wallet more than once. In fact, you will lose it so many times you will feel as if you've lost your mind. I could write an entire chapter simply by listing things I have lost over the past six decades.

Then there are the things you lose that knock the breath out of you. You may lose your job. Your career. Your home, your wealth, your symbols of success. Quite often those losses come with massive implications. It's not just the possessions, it's losing your hope for the future and everything you have worked so hard to achieve. Sometimes the losses are intangible. You can just as quickly watch fame, power, or status disappear. Perhaps you used to be somebody, and now you feel as if you are nobody.

Most of us understand that these losses are possible. Insurance companies make their living off of our fear of losing what we have. Fear is a powerful driver, and more often than not, it's the fear of not having that drives us to have more.

"More of what?" then becomes the critical question. If we don't know what really matters, we will spend our lives accumulating the very things that do not matter—discarding the things that matter most.

There is a subtle evolution of value that we all experience throughout childhood, adolescence, and adulthood. Our priorities change, but hopefully they also mature.

When we are children, life is all about things. That's why Christmas and birthdays are the most important days of the year. If you've ever watched children playing together, you have likely seen evidence of this mindset: No matter how many toys fill the space, the toy most children want is the one other children are playing with. It is a fascinating—and sad—study in human nature to witness ten three-year-olds in a classroom all fighting for one toy while dozens of other toys surround them, completely ignored.

My son, Aaron, was around five years old when I took one of my first trips to Asia. We were very close, and he wasn't accustomed to my being gone from home for so long. We would talk on the phone, and with every passing day, he would tell me how much he missed me and plead with me to come home. Even now, we are as close as a father and son can be.

Midway through that trip, he asked that I please come home "now!" I explained that I couldn't leave because I still had a few more days of work. He began to appeal with more emotion than usual, insisting that I return right away. I kept explaining that that simply wasn't possible. When he finally relented, having realized that he could not change my schedule, he paused, took a breath, and then presented a compromise: "Well, if you can't come home right now will you at least send my present?"

Personally, I thought this was hilarious. I shared this story years later, when my son was an adult, and Aaron said, "Dad, I don't know if you should share this. That story makes me sound like a horrible person." I responded, "No, you're a wonderful person. It makes you sound like a child. Which is exactly what you were." For the first dozen years of our lives, life really is about things. We all have to learn to share. We all have to grow to see the other child and not just the toy.

Eventually, we grow out of this stage. At least we're supposed to. Sadly, I've met countless fifty-year-olds who still obsess over what they don't have and what someone else does. It can be as subtle as caring more about your house looking perfect than whether your kids feel at home in it. It can be as commonplace as sneaking glances at your cell phone and ignoring the person in the room. It can be as psychological as asking "Is the car okay?" when hearing that your teenage son had an accident. It can be as shallow as buying high-fashion brands to gain others' approval rather than because you love the product. It can be as addictive as buying the bigger house or car or plane because your personal value and identity are defined by what you own.

In these scenarios, the person's value system never changed—all that changed was the size and price tag of the things they made their priorities. For them, life is still about trying to get whatever toy someone else has in their hands.

The best way to lose your life and look back with regret is to never mature past the mindset that life is all about things. We need to be careful that we've not simply replaced fighting over the LEGOs in the nursery with fighting over who has the most Lamborghinis. We cannot accumulate enough things to make our lives worth living.

Eventually, most of us transition into the second stage of development. For people in this stage, life is no longer about things but about experiences. Often it's filled with firsts. Our first crush. Our first date. Our first kiss. Our first taste of independence. Life revolves around every new experience, and they make us feel alive.

Those experiences are not inconsequential. They shape our identity and self-worth. We want the experience of winning, so we play football. We want to be popular, so we join the cheer team. We want to be loved, so we experience sexual intimacy long before we're ready for it. After all, life is all about experiences. If we're not experiencing, we're not living. At least that's what we think.

Eventually, we begin to see life a bit differently. Having nice things makes life nice, and great experiences can enrich us and leave us with wonderful memories. But eventually we realize that possessions and experiences are enhancements to life, not its ultimate meaning. This epiphany is perhaps the singular transition that moves us from adolescence into adulthood. When we grasp that life is about people, when we make people our highest priority, this shift becomes the best measure of maturity, wholeness, and health.

I have a friend who amassed a net worth of nearly fifty million dollars by the time he was in his thirties. I met him through a Mastermind group that he leads with one of his business partners—a think tank and investment community for people whose companies are worth minimally one hundred million dollars. As we talked about how I could contribute, he suggested an unexpected direction. He explained that at least seven of his close friends who were CEOs had filed for divorce that year. He encouraged me that if I had the time and energy, one of the greatest contributions I could make was to help successful entrepreneurs navigate the tumultuous waters of making their marriages work.

I've seen this challenge up close as I've counseled couples whose marriages were struggling and even falling apart. I cannot even begin to describe the brutal complexity of two people fighting over assets, properties, and children—the life they've built together. The devastation can be immeasurable when two people who once loved each other now feel nothing but bitterness and hate. They can gain the whole world, have extraordinary experiences, make beautiful memories together, and in the process of achieving the unimaginable in their work and career, end up losing the people who matter most to them.

This is exactly why some companies have divorce clauses among their founding members, even when the spouses have nothing to do with the company. If a founding partner files for divorce, they are obligated to sell their shares at the current market value, protecting the organization from any fallout in the divorce. Even a company whose only priority is the value of their stock understands that a marriage gone bad creates devastation far beyond the two people involved. How much more should we understand the interconnection between our private and public selves?

In writing this chapter, I have made a basic assumption about you as the reader. If you're reading this book, it's likely that you are a type A personality—or at least want to act like one. You are driven. You are focused on your goals, ambitions, and dreams. You are relentless in your pursuit of excellence and achieving personal greatness. You may even struggle with the feeling that people hold you back and slow you down. If any of this resonates, you need to be cognizant of the fact that when we focus on our goals, the people in our life may quickly go out of focus.

I have friends who made the conscious choice to put their relationships on the back burner while they built their personal empire. There is a lot to be said about that kind of intentionality.

The danger, of course, is that you can become blind to the importance of the people in your life. No one succeeds alone. Yet some people take all the credit for the success in their lives. Success is far richer, more meaningful, and more sustainable when you build it in the context of healthy relationships. People must never be a means to an end. Relationships should never be simply utilitarian.

When I asked Mark Burnett, the producer of shows like *Survivor* and *Shark Tank,* to tell me the key for his sustainable success, he didn't talk about his creative process or the individual genius that has helped him create smash-hit programs for more than twenty years. Instead he described the small, loyal, tight-knit team that moves with him whenever he takes on a new endeavor. When your strategy for success includes the people in your life who are willing to join you and pay the price with you, it is immeasurably more rewarding.

My brother, Alex, recently came to LA from Detroit to work on a project with me. He's my older brother by twenty months, a brilliant thinker and gifted teacher. While we were catching up at dinner with two of our Mosaic Learning Labs instructors, he gave me the greatest compliment possible. He said, "You're the most generous person I know. I don't mean only with money, even though that's true too. I mean you're the most generous person with opportunities. I've never known anyone so intent on creating space and opportunity for others."

It's a bit awkward for me to write this down and share it with you, but it reflects one of my highest values. I have never measured my success by how much I've accomplished, or how much I have acquired. I have always measured my success by how many people I can take with me on the journey. My measure is simple: Do people elevate when they are in the gravitational pull of my life? Am I investing in the success of others? When you make the mind shift that it's not all about you—it's all about the people whose lives change for the better because of you—it is transformational.

What does this shift look like in practice? It's choosing to be kind. It's tipping well when people serve you.

It's taking time to acknowledge the people around you and remember their names. It's speaking well of people when they are not in the room. It's remembering who helped you when you needed them, and returning the favor. It's making time for friendship. It's refusing to have the mentality that it's not personal, it's just business. It's making sure it's *always* personal. It's listening. It's being present. It's seeing life through the template of relationships.

When you finally understand that life is all about people, everything in your life changes.

If you wait too long to come to this realization, you will find yourself looking back with at least some degree of regret. You will see where you chose things over people and wonder what you were thinking. The things you attained at the cost of the people you genuinely counted as friends were not worth the exchange. Most likely, those things no longer have the value that you perceived they would have, and they certainly did not bring you the happiness you expected.

Experiences are actually quite nuanced. I have an incredible appreciation for great experiences. Yet, what I've come to realize is that the greatest experiences are the ones that are shared. Even the best experiences do not bring us a sense of fulfillment when we experience them alone. After all, what makes for a great experience? What makes it unforgettable? What qualifies it to become a life-long memory? It's not the experience itself. It's the people with whom you shared it.

In November of 2022, I took on my friend's challenge to create a couples' Mastermind event. I carefully curated an experience for ten couples, bringing them together for four days of learning and conversation. Most of them did not know one another, but I knew they had many similar life experiences. The common denominator was that they knew and trusted me and my wife, Kim, and had great respect for our marriage. The sessions were amazing, even life-changing. We began each day with three to four hours of coaching, then we would break for lunch. The rest of the day was open-ended, except we would all come together and share an evening meal.

The sessions became the catalyst for the endless hours of spontaneous conversations, unplanned lunch meetings, and even heated competitive sports that bonded us together. I helped the couples reflect on a series of personal and interpersonal dynamics, such as how they process and make decisions; how much emotional energy they bring to their relationship; whether their mindset as a spouse was win/win, win/lose, or lose/win; and how each person in the relationship tended to respond to stress. Husbands and wives began opening up their lives to each other. Couples began helping one another as they processed the challenges of their own relationships. Even business competitors became collaborators and colleagues. Two of the couples who had never met before the Mastermind extended their stays and spent a few more days together. The experience was over, but the relationships endured.

My point in sharing the story is this: Although these are arguably some of the busiest people in the world, they made time to grow personally, as couples, and as friends. Earlier today, one of the couples who'd been at the retreat dropped by our house unexpectedly to express how grateful they were for that time. If relationships are your highest value, you will make time to nourish them and invest in them.

If I could say anything to my twenty-five-year-old self, it would be this: Never choose things or experiences over relationships. It may take some time, but find your people and do life together. I am so grateful I didn't have to go through cancer alone. I am grateful that my career successes were shared with teams that I loved so much, people who had a hand in creating the success. Even when I win at basketball, it's more rewarding when my friends are there to witness the magic while it's happening. Life is richer with good people in your life. *You* are richer with good people in your life.

Still, even when you are surrounded by good people, things are not necessarily easy. Many people will come in and out of your life who are actually not your people. It's not that they do not have value or importance in your journey; they're simply not the people who will travel with you to the very end. You may be seasonal in some people's lives, and they might be in your life for only a season as well.

There will be hard choices to make along the journey. If you choose a life of continuous progress, you will lose more people from your life than you will keep. You will find that some people love you for who you are but not for who you are becoming. We will address those challenges in the chapters to come. But before we get there, you need to establish this principle in your life: Life is about relationships. Even when you have all the possessions you desire and have experienced every great adventure, broken relationships will steal the joy from it all. The greatest mistakes you will ever make will not cost you money; they will cost you people.

You Don't Need an Audience

He shook me frantically. His words seemed a thousand miles away as he leaned so close to my face that I could feel both his breath and his panic. Twenty thousand students were converging into Dallas Arena to hear a speaker who hadn't shown up. Unless I was in a deep sleep and this conversation was just a dream, it was time for me to panic as well.

The executive director of the event was giving me the opportunity of a lifetime. He needed someone to fill the headliner's shoes, and for some reason, he had decided to pass over the dozen or more professional speakers waiting in that same room. Every one of them was dressed in a tailored suit, and there I was in blue jeans, tennis shoes, and a pullover shirt.

At twenty-nine years old, I had never spoken to more

than two hundred people in my life. In fact, two hundred would have been a lot. Most of the time I spoke to rooms of several dozen. Now here I was, in the green room of a stadium event, with a man telling me that he needed me to step up and address the waiting crowd.

I started to laugh. He had an entire entourage of prominent speakers in the queue just waiting for a moment like this. I hadn't even planned on being there. My wife, Kim, worked as an administrative assistant for the organization in charge of the event. I was there as her volunteer, a backstage hand. I was David, the giant slayer, delivering cheese to the front line, not a warrior dressed to fight Goliath. This man couldn't be serious. Based on the heated conversations we'd had in the past, he didn't even like me. Surely he was just messing with me, hoping I would take the bait and say yes, only to be told I would be his last choice on earth.

But he wasn't kidding. I don't remember saying yes. I just remember saying, "I'll need a Bible." He responded without hesitation, "What translation?" And we were off to the races. I would have less than sixty minutes to prepare for the most important message of my life.

To add to the pressure, some random person walked up to me right then and said, "This is your moment. This is the moment that will mark your life and your future." To this day, I'm not sure if he said it to encourage me or terrify me. I wanted to puke. I thought, *Is this the moment I want to be my moment? Do I even know how to hold cap-*

tive an audience of this size? Is this man out of his mind choosing to trust me with a moment of such magnitude?

But that stranger was exactly right—that day did mark my life and my future. I will never forget it.

If you are a speaker, you know when an audience is with you. You know when there is a transcendent connection between you and everyone in the seats. In that moment you are not speaking to a crowd of twenty thousand but to each person directly and intimately. Somehow, the moment I stepped onto that platform, I felt as if I belonged there. There was something inside of me that told me I was made for this.

I will never forget what I spoke on that night: character that does not compromise. I talked about how courage was the defining virtue all of us needed to be fully alive. Without courage, we will never have the character to live out our guiding principles and relentlessly pursue our highest calling. When I finished my message, I invited any and all who would choose to step into the life they were created to live to come to the stage and respond to that call. Thousands of students stepped away from their seats as far as the upper decks, flooding the stage, desperate for change. For the next hour, counselors were overwhelmed by the masses whose lives had been impacted by an address from someone whose name they didn't even know.

In the decades since, I have met people who still attribute the direction of their lives to that night and the message I had the privilege of presenting. And while I have come to know of thousands of lives changed that evening, what I'm certain of is that one life that changed forever was mine.

That conference opened up the world to me as a speaker. It was the pivotal event in a journey that would lead me to reach millions across seventy countries over the past thirty-five years. It also taught me to always be prepared. Prepare for the unexpected. Prepare to bring your best at a moment's notice. Prepare for the impossible. Prepare for your purpose.

As I look back on the fear I felt in the green room, I now see that there is a difference between not having advance notice and not being prepared. In truth, I had been preparing for that moment for nearly a decade.

Let me give you a bit of backstory. I spent the first half of my twenties finishing up my bachelor's degree from the University of North Carolina at Chapel Hill and completing my master's degree in Fort Worth, Texas. My studies focused on philosophy, psychology, languages, and theology. I was fascinated with the mystery of what makes people do what they do.

I look back now and realize that what I had become was a social anthropologist. What I hadn't become was a public speaker. All of my life I had been extremely introverted, reclusive, and shy. I loved to study people, but I never wanted to stand in front of them and have them study me.

But there was another thread in my life that was more

seminal to my development. It wasn't the years in the classroom that had the greatest impact on me. It was the time I spent working among the urban poor. While studying for my master's, I began working in the downtown streets of Dallas and Fort Worth, helping homeless people to reclaim their lives. Then I took a job in the region of Dallas that had become the zip code with one of the highest crime and murder rates in the United States. I created programs that met basic human needs and helped people develop the skills necessary to live a self-sustaining life. Our organization was faith-based, so most of the people I talked to already claimed to have faith. What they didn't have were the mental structures to create a different life. Although I couldn't change the fact that the poor are rarely given the same advantages, opportunities, or quality of education that are common among those with privilege, I could work to give them what is often readily available to those with more access: a mindset for positive, substantive, and sustainable life change.

My audience consisted of drug dealers, drug addicts, ex-convicts, future convicts, and families trapped in urban poverty. The average reading level was just above third grade. If I was going to help develop the full potential of the people in this fledgling community and help them break out of poverty, it would require that I take concepts that I had learned at the graduate level of education and translate them so that even the most uneducated person could understand them.

My first audiences were not gathered in safe and comfortable auditoriums but on the city streets and in the courtyards of government projects. It's nerve-wracking enough to debate the meaning of life with philosophers and PhDs, but it's a whole other thing to do it with drug dealers and gang members. I would walk into some of the most violent and antagonistic environments in our cities and, through spontaneous conversations, earn the right to be heard. I had to earn not only my audience's attention but my audience, itself.

When I went to work among the urban poor, I assumed all I needed to do was change their hearts. However, I quickly discovered that I also had to change their minds. It was easier for many of the people we worked with to believe in God than it was for them to believe in the critical relationship between cause and effect. Many of them believed success was the consequence of fate or luck or privilege. I began extricating the basic principles that successful and healthy people take for granted. This included simple things, like keep your promises—both to yourself and to others. Make very few promises and replace them with commitments. Finish what you start. Only start what you are willing to finish. Be trustworthy. Be grateful. Be humble. Take responsibility.

I wasn't trying to be a great speaker so I could become well known. I was determined to convince people I came to love that their lives could be different, that they could change to become the best versions of themselves, that there was greatness within them waiting to be awakened. It didn't matter if there were only twenty people in the room. I had to master the frequencies of communication because people's lives depended on it.

So, in retrospect, no—I *wasn't* unprepared for the conference that changed my life. I'd been doing the work for ten years, not knowing where that preparation would take me. In the process, I became both a student and an expert in human behavior and optimal performance.

Sometimes I wonder if that path would have been open to me today. It used to be that you had to earn an audience through years of harnessing and developing your talent, but we no longer live in those times. In this new reality, we first find a way to build an audience, and then we shape ourselves to become what we need to be to keep that audience. Evidently this phenomenon has become so culturally significant that it now has a name: "audience capture." In this scenario, it's not about who you are or what you have accomplished; it's about how others perceive your success. It's not about who you are as a person but who you are as a personality. We believe we have achieved greatness just because people are paying attention to us. But the question becomes, are you capturing an audience or is the audience capturing you?

Several years ago, I went to a TED Conference and was surprised to hear a speaker from Harvard University advocate for the strategic benefit of a "fake it till you make it" approach to success. I understood the intention behind the talk. The idea is that no one starts with all the qualifications they'll need for success, so they should build their brand, and then build themselves to match their brand. It's a strategy many companies and start-ups use today. The problem with this approach is that it's unsustainable when you're talking about the life of a single human being. Once you go public, you are in the pressure cooker. You have an image, but you may not have substance. The psychological energy it takes to pretend to have already arrived while still figuring it out is exhausting, taxing, and potentially self-destructive. You cannot sustain a life built from the outside in.

There is a part of us that feels as if we are faking it to some degree. It has become known as impostor syndrome. I certainly am no different. I never feel as if I deserve to be in the rooms I'm invited into. I'm always surprised when I'm invited to speak. If you never feel good enough or talented enough or prepared enough, welcome to the party. Still, this is different from faking it.

Faking it is not about stretching yourself to accomplish more than you ever have before. It's about convincing others that you are something you know you are not. It's about pretending you have already arrived. And pretending is exhausting. It steals your energy.

Not only is this phenomenon relevant when you are seeking fame from the masses, but it is equally true when you are seeking validation from a few. If your identity and self-worth are shaped more by what others think of you than by internal measures, you will live at the mercy of the opinion of others and never know your true self.

Now, nearly thirty-five years after that event in Dallas, I have spoken to millions of people globally. I've learned that you don't need an audience to prepare for the biggest moments of your life. Commit to greatness when you have no audience. Discipline yourself and prepare yourself to be the best at what you do. Live as if today you may be given the greatest opportunity of your life. Be ready to step up when the call comes.

Fame is what you're known for. Greatness is what you are. You can be great and never be famous. You might be a scientist who discovers the cure for a disease, for example, but science doesn't play well on TikTok, so you may end up living the rest of your life in obscurity. You might be a great mathematician who unlocks the mysteries of the universe and at best become a household name among a handful of physicists. Maybe your grandfather worked the coal mines, or the assembly line, or the front lines, all to create a better life for his children and grandchildren. Is his greatness any less great for the lack of fame?

Here's the key: Don't try to keep up with those who use all their energy pursuing fame. They are on the fast track. You need to play the long game. But know that if you do this, it might not go well for you in the short term. You will be the tortoise, not the hare. You might feel as if you're losing ground while other people are earning more money or attention or living out your dreams.

Stay the course. Greatness takes time. In its earliest stages, it looks like practice. Every great novelist has written millions of words that will never be read. The neurosurgeon with the skills to save your life sacrificed more than a decade of their own life gaining those skills. The tennis great who makes that impossible shot to win Wimbledon hit that same shot a thousand times while training for that championship.

You may think you need an audience to reveal your greatness. The truth is, the audience will sidetrack you from your future. You perform for the audience; you develop for yourself. That's the paradox with unlocking your greatness. While the outcome may gain you the adoration of the masses, the process is a journey you must be willing to walk alone. Greatness is always grown in private. If you want to do what no one has done before, you must be willing to do what no one is doing. Even those close to you will not understand your intensity and the focus essential for continuous improvement. If you need the applause to be great, you will never survive the process. But if you want to move toward your optimal capacity, you must decide that the applause that matters comes from within. The crowd will meet you at the finish line, but your resilience and determination will accompany you the whole way.

Don't pay the price of greatness for the praise of people, the cheers of the crowd, or the adoration of fans. Work in private to be the best. Do the work that no one sees. Do the work so you can look at yourself in the mirror and know you gave it all you had. Do it for yourself, and the audience will take care of itself. When you make a commitment to show up for yourself, you'll be surprised how many people show up for you.

You Can't Take Everyone with You

A few years ago, I was sitting with my wife, Kim, reflecting on one of the most difficult decades of our lives. I had come to a very simple conclusion about the reason behind that struggle. I said to her, "We spent far too much time with people who didn't deserve any of our time."

In my twenties and thirties, I worked for a variety of different organizations, and they all required that I master the skill of developing leaders. But the most challenging job by far was when I attempted to lead a church. When you are a pastor, you are supposed to care about everyone and treat everyone equally—or at least that's how I understood the role. But those good intentions left me with a leadership pyramid that was completely backward. If you wanted my time, all you had to do was complain a lot. If you were 100 percent on board, completely committed to the vision, I didn't have time for you. As a result, I unwittingly encouraged negative behavior.

It was a difficult season in our life. Much of our challenge came from a deep desire to see the church reaching the people we were there to serve. We dreamed of creating a community where those who were searching for God would have a place to belong and explore faith, even if they did not believe. This required radical reinvention for an institution not known for change. The music changed, the dress code changed, the language changed. We brought in the arts and unleashed creativity. We also became one of the most ethnically diverse communities in one of the most racially divided cities in the United States. Previously, our church was an aging community that had been declining for fifteen years. We were a million dollars in debt and a hundred thousand dollars in the red. If we had been a business, we would have already filed for bankruptcy. Within a year of our reinvention, the average age of the congregation was twenty-four years old and our finances began to reflect the growing excitement and commitment of a thriving community of faith. In one moment the church had no future, and in the next, it *was* the future.

Still, there was tremendous resistance to change and growth. Some people saw church as an escape from the outside world, and now their sacred space was filled with strangers who did not look or think like them. I never could have predicted the amount of turmoil and hostility these changes would create. It seemed as if every conversation was either complaints, criticism, or conflict. At the core of every conflict was the struggle between the past and the future. Was the primary responsibility of our institution to preserve the past or create the future? If you're a church, both choices will cost you dearly. One will cost you your traditions, the other your children.

I constantly tried to make everyone happy. I hoped that if I had one more conversation, held one more meeting, gave them more of my time, they would finally come on board. After all, I was just trying to do the right thing. This was a dying organization that would cease to exist if I didn't make the necessary changes. Surely people would see that I was for them, that I was going through all of this chaos and uncertainty for their benefit. Frankly, there were easier jobs available that paid a lot more. I thought that if I couldn't get everyone to see the vision, I must be doing something wrong.

It took me years to realize that the very opposite is true. If everyone agrees with you, you're probably not leading at all.

Leaders create clarity, raise standards, and call people to more. By definition, this creates a dividing line. Great leaders are not afraid to define what it means to be on their team, organization, or movement. They know their vision isn't for everyone, and they recognize those with a shared vision. Great leaders also know that great teams form when there is a sifting process.

For years I allowed those most resistant to change to

have the most influence on our rate, pace, and scale of transformation—even though this went completely against my natural inclination. I was an idealist. I genuinely valued people, and I thought that meant that I should act as if every person could thrive in our new reality. What I didn't realize is that most institutions—whether they're a church or a Fortune 100 company—are led by administrators and managers. Their highest value is to protect what exists. Their strength is risk management. Their weakness is an aversion to innovation, creativity, and risk.

This is even truer if you're a second-generation company. The entrepreneurs who found such organizations tend to be agents of change. Their personalities are designed for creating, but rarely for maintaining. Often, after the founder has retired or been removed, the company must search for someone who can bring order to the chaos. After a few iterations of the same process, movements turn into institutions. Over time, the people who are placed in power tend to be those who are most resistant to change. Their instinct is to protect the institution. They see innovators as a threat to stability. The kiss of death for any company is when late adopters have secured control over the organization.

This is especially true when you're leading a nonprofit or a church. It's one thing to have an executive board full of late adopters; it's another thing to have a congregation with five hundred of them. But time and experience have taught me that you can't take everyone with you. I've learned through great pain and loss that transitions are a natural and even healthy exit for those who want an alternative future than the one you are creating.

Twelve years ago, we relocated Mosaic to the heart of Hollywood. The move seemed like a no-brainer. It's a rare opportunity to get to plant your flag on Hollywood Boulevard, a place where millions of people visit every year. We had multiple campuses across Los Angeles, and our most established campus at the time was in massive flux. With no permanent location, we were constantly having to relocate our services at a moment's notice. We had to move more than two thousand people back and forth between Pasadena and then Glendale and then back to Pasadena. The property on Hollywood Boulevard would give our community a home, a place where we could invite Angelenos to come and find meaning and hope.

Still, it became a significant leadership challenge. If you don't live in LA, you cannot fully grasp how much Angelenos hate Hollywood. The glitz and glamour are an illusion. There are no stars or celebrities who actually live in La La Land. Hollywood is a tourist trap. It is run-down, decaying, and overrun with crime and out-of-towners. If you live in LA, you simply do not go to Hollywood for anything. However, the vast majority of Mosaic had the posture that they would go wherever they needed to go to have the greatest impact on our city. Still, it was a lot to ask, even from a logistical standpoint.

One evening, Kim was assessing the cost of what this

move would entail. She began naming one, then two, then three families she felt certain we would lose. By then, I was no longer a novice to the leadership journey. I understood the costs of change. I also understood that without change, there is no future. As a leader, you cannot make decisions based on who you have. You have to make decisions based on who you serve.

Kim named three of our most-committed families. These three families had been with us for decades. They had served in the church alongside us and become our personal friends. I felt the pain of losing them at a gut level. Although Kim didn't mean to do this, I sensed she was holding it against me. *I* was holding it against me. After a moment of silence, I shared with her a harsh reality that I will never forget: "I wish I had the luxury of making my decisions based on only three families. I have the responsibility to make decisions based on the thousands of families that *will* be affected."

I've worked with thousands of companies, nonprofit organizations, and churches over the years, and this phenomenon is a constant. Your leadership will not only gain people, it will also lose people. In fact, at first, you will be more defined by who you lose than by who you gain.

I hope you never take this reality lightly. There is no higher cost than people. But what you will realize over time is that not everyone belongs to your vision. If you're a football coach and your vision is to transition the offense to a run-oriented playbook, you may lose your passing quarterback and your best receivers in the off-season. No matter how much you've committed to integrating them into the new system, they simply don't fit your direction for the organization. Likewise, if you purchased FOX News Channel with the vision of making it left-leaning politically, you would face tremendous internal turmoil and opposition, no matter how diplomatic or magnanimous you tried to be in the transition.

Having people choose to leave can be the greatest gift they give to you. Some of your most defining moments will be when you bring such clarity that people know whether they are in or out. In the process, you help them define their values. They may not choose to move forward with you, but they may be choosing to move forward with their lives.

Thirty years in, Mosaic has become a beautiful community that took decades to nurture and grow. We aren't for everyone. There are great places for those who value tradition and ritual and a small community of family and friends. Our great reward has been to witness hundreds of thousands of people across the world find in us a place to believe and belong and become.

Even though I've come to understand this, losing people has still been a hard pill to swallow. I lost people I never wanted to lose. I lost people I liked. I lost people I loved. I lost people who I thought would be there to the very end. I cannot tell you how many times I heard the phrase, "We are here to stay." However, over time, I dis-

covered that it was one of the best predictors that someone would one day leave. The ones who never leave don't
need to say it. They just show up, no matter how hard the
journey has become.

All of this has taught me the importance of building
your inner circle. You might think the supporters and co-
workers you are closest with now will become permanent
fixtures in your life. But that is not always the case. In
fact, early on, you may not have full control over who
that inner circle contains. You may be brought on as a
CEO, but you did not choose your board. You may be the
head coach, but you did not choose the players or the
management. You may be a pastor, but you did not
choose your elders or deacons.

This is why it is so important to choose the people
with whom you do life. You need a personal inner circle.
You need people you trust. People who believe in you.
People who are not only committed to your vision but
also committed to you. People you are committed to with
the same level of honesty and support. This is the crew
that's going to carry you through your most difficult moments. This is the crew that's bound to you through
blood, sweat, and tears. Sometimes they're a part of your
formal organization and sometimes they are outliers.

Whatever else you do, make sure you find your people, and keep that circle tight and true. And here's the
most difficult part to accept: Many of them may be seasonal in your life, as you are in theirs.

For your inner circle to stay with you for a lifetime, one of two things needs to happen: You either all need to remain the same or all need to keep growing together. If you make a lifelong decision to always keep growing, there is a higher likelihood that those who were deeply committed to you in one season of your life will not choose to join you for the next part of your journey. These will be the most difficult losses of your life. But these losses will also be the product of the most important choices you will ever make.

Always make room for people to go with you into your future, but never sacrifice your future for those who want you to stay exactly how you are. You need people in your life who will cheer you on as you risk and grow. You need people in your life who will celebrate your success. I'm grateful that I have friends like that in my life. Friends who challenge me to push the limits of my faith and capacity. Friends who believe in me more than I believe in myself. I know they are reading this right now, and they know exactly who they are.

Don't spend your time trying to lead people who don't want to go with you. And never try to coerce people to follow you. It never works and never lasts. Paint a picture of a future that seems impossible and yet compels you to try to create it, and know that there will be people who also carry that dream within them. You are the voice that gives sound to the vision, but each person must embrace the vision for themselves.

If the hardest seasons of my life have taught me one thing about the complex reality of relationships, it is this: You can't take everyone with you. Choose people who choose the future. Choose friends who are committed to living at the highest level, and who will challenge you to do the same.

MIND SHIFT #4:

They Won't Get It
Until You Do It

I was sitting backstage waiting my turn to be interviewed for a TV show. The guest who went before me was a renowned expert in leadership, someone whose books I read when developing my own philosophy. I was intently listening in as the host interviewed this man, extracting insights from his life and experience.

At one point, he used a metaphor that captured my attention. His advice to young leaders was, "Never be the first to eat the mushrooms." He explained that long ago, early indigenous people would forage for mushrooms as a source of nutrition. The challenge, of course, was that some mushrooms kept you alive and others would kill you. I must admit, I would not be able to tell the difference between a poisonous mushroom and a shiitake if I had them both sitting in front of me. It's a good thing I was born in the twentieth century.

The guest continued his explanation. "Whoever eats the mushroom first is the one who's going to die." His leadership advice: "Never be the one who goes first." Let someone else eat the mushroom. Let someone else take the risk. Once you know the mushrooms are edible and safe, then you can eat them and enjoy. The guy who eats second has the competitive advantage.

It would be my turn to speak in just a few minutes. I had prepared my thoughts before coming to the studio, but suddenly I could hardly remember my talking points. I couldn't shake the other guest's metaphor. Here was one of my leadership heroes giving advice that my instincts told me was completely wrong. I mean, he was not wrong in the most fundamental of ways. It is safer, more logical, more reasonable and responsible to wait until someone else eats the first mushroom. After all, if you're the one who survives, you'll be the one who gets the credit, even if you didn't take the risk.

As the guest walked off the stage and I began to walk on, we greeted each other, cordially acknowledging the positive impact we'd had on each other through our writings. I must confess, I felt deeply honored that he even knew I existed. But there was little time to reflect on that. I was now in front of the camera and the hot studio lights.

The host began by asking me the same question. What was my philosophy or approach toward leadership? I began by acknowledging the admiration I had for the previous guest. Then I thanked him for something unexpected. I told the host that I had just found my life metaphor. I was a mushroom eater.

I acknowledged that there was wisdom in going second. But as I thought about that metaphor, I explained, a simple question kept haunting me: What if no one goes first? What if everyone waits to mitigate their risk by going second? I couldn't get behind the idea that those who went first did it out of ignorance or obliviousness to their own safety. Perhaps they did it because they made a fundamental decision that their lives were not as important as what their sacrifice could bring to the whole. Someone has to eat the mushrooms first, or else everyone will die of hunger. If no one goes first, there is no future. If no one goes first, we all die.

The world is changed by the mushroom eaters. Humanity has advanced through the courage and sacrifice of the pioneers, adventurers, explorers, and innovators. If you are playing it safe, you are playing to lose. The full measure of your gifts, and talents, and potential, and life, cannot be actualized if you are not willing to step into risk.

Too many of us are playing the imitation game. We spend much of our lives making decisions that we believe others want us to make. Sometimes, our motivations are really close to home. You're trying to become the son your father wanted you to be. You're trying to become the daughter that your parents feel they deserve. You're trying to live up to your name or the hopes of those closest to you. Our lives are not created in a vacuum. We are born into a world of expectations. A huge part of self-leadership is breaking away from the gravitational pull of the opinions of others and finding the courage to become the most unique version of you.

Just today I spoke with a former professional athlete who was working as a sports agent. He absolutely hated it. Two different NBA teams had offered him jobs working with players, and he needed to make a decision about his future. When I asked him what he wanted to do, he surprised me. His answer had nothing to do with sports. Instead, he said that he loved real estate. He was already beginning the process to get his broker's license.

This is a great example of how one person's dream is another person's nightmare. Someone else would have given anything to work in the NBA or be a sports agent, but this guy wanted nothing more than to buy and sell houses. I see this all the time. An engineer who wants to become an artist. A lawyer who dreams of becoming an actor. An actor who fantasizes about becoming a rancher. A teacher who becomes a chef.

Now, maybe you are not a risk taker. Maybe you don't feel called or compelled to become an explorer or pioneer or innovator, and definitely not a willing martyr. That's okay. This mind shift still applies to you on a very personal level.

It takes great courage for any of us to become the person we're created to be. Forget changing history—how about changing yourself? It takes courage to live a life of integrity and intention. It takes courage to live a life of compassion. It takes courage to live a life of generosity. It takes courage to love.

Why is it that our creating a new future or becoming a new and better version of ourself is so difficult, even for those who love us? It's simple. One thing we cannot see is the future—especially someone else's. Could anyone see who Elon Musk would become? Or Jeff Bezos? Or Bill Gates? Or Oprah Winfrey? Could anyone have imagined what these people would create with their lives? The future is the territory of mystery and uncertainty. To travel into your future means choosing to leave the safety of the past and the present. Oddly enough, the people who love you most may be the most terrified when you decide to leave what you have for what you long for.

When you share your vision or dream with those around you, don't be surprised if they try to discourage you from pursuing such insanity. Although you will want them to see the possibilities of your dream, most will see the problems: There is no way you will ever harness electricity; No one will ever buy groceries online; Manufacturing electric cars is absurd—where are they going to charge them? You will never succeed.

You may begin to wonder if you are out of your mind. Others will ask you, Why can't you be satisfied with the life you have? Why can't you cooperate and accept the status quo? We like you as you are; why do you need to change? These questions may all come from sincere people with good intentions, but it goes to show that most new ideas face great opposition.

You must choose between acceptance and uniqueness. If you're addicted to affirmation, you will become a reflection of yourself rather than the genuine version of you. It may seem a bit overdramatic, but this really is a matter of life or death. Or at the very least, a matter of life or existence.

Before the pandemic, I spoke at a gathering of a few hundred millionaires and billionaires who all were involved in some form of philanthropy. When I arrived, I was unaware that I actually knew the man who put together this unique group of high achievers. At the dinner table, he looked strangely familiar. It wasn't long before I realized we'd actually met twenty years earlier. The host never mentioned it, so I assumed he did not remember me. That would not have been surprising; I was not a person of consequence when we met all those years ago.

Just before it was my moment to speak, the man stepped up to the stage to introduce me. I expected the classic introduction, with someone reading a few complimentary lines about my work. That wasn't at all what happened. He introduced me by telling the story of when we met. He remembered me as a young man who had a dream, who secured a meeting with him in hopes that he would invest a small part of his immense wealth to help make it happen.

I remember that meeting so clearly. I had been told that this man loved investing in new ideas and that he was a very generous person. I drove several hours outside of Dallas to meet him, thinking about my pitch the whole way. We ate Chinese food. I don't know why that stands out to me, but it does. When I finished my presentation— which, by the way, he graciously listened to completely— I sat there awkwardly awaiting his response.

He was very straightforward and did not mince words. He simply responded, "I'm not going to invest in your idea. I don't believe it's possible." But before he showed me the door, he added something that I've never forgotten. He said, "I've rarely met anyone with so much passion. It's rare to meet someone with passion. Even more rare to meet someone as passionate as you."

I drove away with zero start-up money. In that sense, the meeting was a complete failure. But on the long drive home, I couldn't stop thinking about our conversation— not the part when he told me he would not invest in my idea, but the moment when he said it's rare to meet a person with so much passion. I thought, *I just met a billionaire, and he told me I was rare. What an incredible gift I've walked away with. If I want to remain rare, I must never lose my passion. You can take away my wealth, but you cannot take away my uniqueness.* That was a life lesson I've carried with me to this day.

Now, here was that same man, on a stage introducing the person he chose not to fund twenty years earlier. He explained to the room that I had pitched him an image of the future and laid out a plan for how to impact it. "Twenty years ago, I couldn't see it," he said. However, he had followed my life over the decades and was astonished to see my dream become a reality. "Twenty years ago, I was wrong. Over the last twenty years, our speaker has proved through his life that his vision for the future was right."

Never surrender your uniqueness for acceptance. On your journey to becoming who you were meant to be, no one can eat the mushroom for you. You must choose to go first. You must choose to take the risk. You must choose to break away from the gravitational pull of expectations. If you are required to be anyone except yourself to be accepted, the price is too high.

As I look back on my life, I was almost always about twenty years early for most of my ideas to be recognized as valid. But if I had waited on validation to act, I would have been twenty years too late. The future is never created on time. If you're fortunate, you may live long enough to see your innovation validated within your lifetime. But it is never about being right. It's about creating the future people need most.

Take the time to figure out who you want to become. Take the time to nurture your own dreams. Make the choices necessary to create the future you long for, and don't expect others to understand the path you have chosen. They won't get it until they see it. You won't see it until you get after it.

You must become the proof of the validity of your vision. Don't wait for the crowd to cheer you on. Don't wait for the applause. Don't wait for everyone to understand what you're doing. Just go and eat the mushroom. Eventually, when everyone is sitting around enjoying their salads, they will thank you for the shiitakes.

You Are Your Own Ceiling

If you've lived long enough, you have already figured this out: Life is hard. None of us gets to choose where we start. Depending on your circumstances, you may feel like you have more obstacles than opportunities ahead of you. I do not want to diminish the reality of some of the challenges you may have already faced in your life.

However, as real as those obstacles may be, it's also true that some of the steepest obstacles in your life will come from within. We all tell ourselves a story: I'm too damaged to ever be healed; I've made too many mistakes to make something of my life; I just can't get a break; I would have accomplished so much if others hadn't held me down; I'm not talented enough to do something significant with my life; I don't have enough money to create wealth; I'm the victim of an unfair system; I'm too young to take on so much responsibility; I'm too old to start over again. The self-limiting stories we tell ourselves are endless.

If you describe your life using all the obstacles that keep you from living up to your potential, you will convince yourself that the reason you have such a low ceiling is that you were born with such a great disadvantage. But if you see all those obstacles as opportunities, you will write a very different story of your life. In the end, what becomes clear is that you are your own ceiling.

Early in my life, I felt as if nothing worked out in my favor. I would compare myself to my talented, intelligent siblings and always find myself falling short. In *A Knight's Tale,* Heath Ledger's character is told, "You have been weighed, you have been measured, and you have been found wanting." That was my life story. I definitely saw life as being unfair. I had good reason.

I'm an immigrant from El Salvador, a country that has become the global standard for violence and murder. At age five, I was dragged off to the United States, a country whose language I did not speak. It's no small thing to be five years old and feel that you don't belong in the world. But that wasn't even the whole of it. I never knew my real father. My grandparents raised me for the first years of my life. My mom worked herself to the bone, hoping that she'd be able to reunite us one day. Still, none of that explained my sense that life was unfair. That feeling was all about me. I never felt that I was enough—good enough, smart enough, gifted enough.

I was a straight D student from first through twelfth grades. On my last day of high school, my English teacher asked if I'd thought about going to college. I said, "Maybe." She replied, "You will never make it." All my life, I felt like I was trapped in a box. I was desperate to break free. I couldn't see that while factors outside of my control may have helped build the box, in the end I was the one who sealed it shut. I blamed the world. I blamed my mom. I blamed God. It was all a blame game. I was angry. I was bitter. I was depressed. I felt powerless. I felt invisible. I felt dead inside. I kept waiting for someone to break me out of the box. It took me a while before I realized that the box was in my mind. I built that box as a way of limiting my responsibility. After all, if someone else was to blame, then it wasn't my fault, and someone else was responsible for fixing it.

It may sound unfair, but it doesn't matter if it's not your fault. It's still your responsibility. No one but you is accountable for your life.

Your brain will tell you that some external factor is holding you back. It's a tempting thought, especially when you're trying to make sense of failure. But when you abdicate responsibility, you relinquish your power. If your circumstances are completely someone else's or something else's fault, then it also means you are powerless to

ERWIN RAPHAEL MCMANUS

change them. The questions we should be asking ourselves are: Where *is* it my responsibility? Where did I fail?
What could I have done differently? You don't want to
internalize failure, but you absolutely want to internalize
responsibility. Where does your thinking need to change?

The height of your ceiling is the perfect reflection of
your mental toughness. You will know you are mentally
tough when your optimal performance is completely unaffected by your environment. If it doesn't take much to
make you quit, your ceiling is going to be unbearably low.
But the good news is that most limitations are illusions
created by our inner fears, doubts, and insecurities. It requires a mind shift to see that the ceiling is not actually
there.

Every day I meet people who are living proof that
limitations are predominantly internal, not external. For
example, there is Edwin, who is Colombian and watched
as his parents were dragged off to state prison when he
was around six years old. Edwin committed his life to
helping people live in homes safe from crime and violence. He is now the owner and CEO of one of the largest
home security companies in the United States.

There is Jamie, a Denny's waitress who never knew her
biological parents and struggled with a skin condition
called rosacea. Her dream was to work in front of a camera and to help women feel their value and beauty. She
became an on-air reporter, and then the founder of a
billion-dollar cosmetic company. She now works as an

author and voice for women's empowerment, helping women feel the same sense of confidence that she sought for herself.

There is Brad, whose wife became pregnant while he was a struggling entrepreneur. She told him, "You have nine months to find an idea that will pay the bills, or you become Mr. Mom." He developed an app that helps people fund their dreams and launched a revolution of grassroot entrepreneurs, activists, and humanitarians, raising the funding they desperately need to fulfill their missions.

Ed grew up with an alcoholic father. He had to decide if he could psychologically recover from the brokenness and abuse that came from a home marked by addiction. Could he break his family's cycles of addiction and poverty and achieve the impossible? Today he is a self-made billionaire, with a podcast that reaches millions of listeners and a book that launched as a bestseller.

Every ceiling someone else places over your potential is a false ceiling. It only exists if you allow it to define you. You have a choice in life: You can spend your life blaming others for where your life is, or you can take responsibility for life and make your future different from your past.

One of the realities of being an ethnic minority is that others will try to place all sorts of assumptions and limitations on you. When my brother, Alex, first moved to Los Angeles he met with a leader who was struggling with his own effectiveness. In their very first meeting, the leader made what he thought was an obvious observation: "As you know, Latins can't lead." It was an odd thing to say to my brother, since he was born in El Salvador. But when you have the last name McManus, it's amazing how many people become oblivious to your ethnicity.

I soon discovered that the man's view of Latinos was not an individual perspective but a commonly held view among many organizational leaders across the country. Not everyone said it quite as bluntly, but the negative assumptions were always there.

Later, I had a meeting with that same person's boss. We had begun working together on a project that I had been asked to lead, and we were sitting together in his car when he decided to put me in my place. "I am more strategic than you will ever be," he said. He attempted to convince me that he was my leadership ceiling, that I could not succeed without him. I think he was genuinely trying to help me. He didn't want me to overreach. He wanted me to stay within myself. He believed he was genetically superior and that I would be leading from a deficit. I never argued with him. I've always found these kinds of arguments to be unproductive. Besides, I have also found there is a great strategic advantage in being underestimated.

This wasn't the first time someone tried to define my leadership ceiling, and it certainly wouldn't be the last. I was once asked to join a national executive team of Hispanics and Latinos brought together to create a national strategy for serving our constituency. It astonished me when the organization selected a chairman who was not Hispanic or Latino. When I pointed out what seemed more than obvious, they made it clear that none of us were qualified to lead at that level.

But there were other times when the limiting assumptions weren't so obvious. In college I was offered a scholarship for being an immigrant from El Salvador. It was a minority scholarship to help Hispanic students achieve their educational goals—which was a wonderful thing. I am grateful to the generous people who make such financial aid possible. But I remember asking what the requirements of the scholarship were, and feeling patronized when they said the scholarship only required that I was Hispanic. I turned it down. I had been raised differently than that. You didn't take anything you didn't earn. (Now, if I had known how many times my immigrant status would become a deficit in the years ahead, I probably would have changed my mind! But I wouldn't trade my mindset for anything.)

Over the years, I have worked with thousands of individuals who were painfully unfulfilled and desperate for change. Some I've known for nearly all my life, and many more I've known for at least half my life. I've learned that a high percentage of people eventually settle for a self-limiting ceiling. Whether it's a relationship ceiling, a leadership ceiling, or a capacity ceiling, the story is very much the same. People hit a wall and they become convinced that they are incapable of going past it. More friends than

I can count started the book they felt compelled to write but never finished it. Others had great ideas for a business but never believed enough in their dreams. Others were incredibly talented people who hated their jobs but settled for the security of a paycheck. Sometimes it was more about personal well-being. Other times it was that they gave up on their health and fitness because they decided they could never change their lifestyle. There are all kinds of ceilings we choose to accept in our lives.

I'm not saying it's easy to break through those limitations. Ceilings can come with tremendous weight. Some can only be removed through intense training and personal development. Others simply require the confidence and courage to believe you're capable of more. Whatever the case, and no matter how many people you have cheering you on, you have to decide that the ceiling is an illusion, not a permanent limitation.

When I say illusion, I do not mean there are not real competencies you must develop in order to get results. I simply mean that the limitations aren't permanent. They are not what's keeping you from elevating to a higher level. The ceiling simply reveals what your next challenge is. It can be your boundary or your calling. You decide. When you hit the proverbial wall, that's when you know it's time to step up and become stronger. To keep elevating throughout your life you need more than mental toughness, you need mental agility. You need the ability to see things in a new way and to solve problems in a new way. Our ceilings are created by our own mental rigidity. When you change your thinking you blow the lid off.

I have never known a successful person who did not build their skyscraper of success one floor at a time. The difference was that they knew their first floor was just that—not the ceiling, but the floor to the next level. Granted, outside factors can make it harder to succeed, and certainly some people have life leveraged in their favor, but it's your inner world that determines your limits. When you take responsibility for your life, you reclaim your power.

MIND SHIFT #6:

Talent Is a Hallucinogen

Out here in Los Angeles, it's all the rage to go on a spiritual pilgrimage using ayahuasca, a hallucinogenic tea that causes altered states of consciousness. For centuries, the tea has been used by indigenous people in the Amazon for sacred purposes. More recently, it has come into the American mainstream, with everyone from medical researchers to NFL quarterback Aaron Rodgers touting its healing properties when it comes to symptoms of depression, grief, and post-traumatic stress. I know quite a few highly educated people who have gone on spiritual quests in South America in hopes that ayahuasca would help them achieve a heightened consciousness that traditional faith hasn't provided.

Whether it's for psychological, emotional, or spiritual transformation, the popularity of ayahuasca is a reminder that we humans are on a desperate search to find healing and wholeness. Beyond that, we are searching for a pathway to unlock our untapped potential and achieve an optimal state of performance. What I find fascinating is whether a hallucination can change you when you return to reality.

We live in a world of hallucinations and illusions. This is especially true when it comes to our beliefs about failure and success. In the last chapter, I wrote that we have a tendency to create false narratives about our limitations as a way of absolving ourselves from our role in our own story. But it's also possible for us to overestimate our latent strengths. We bet on talent, overlook character, and underestimate grit. It's why we are confused when we see someone underachieving, despite having all the inborn skills and advantages in the world.

I say all of this to get to one critical point: Talent is a hallucinogen.

Talent creates an illusion of success. It causes you to believe a false reality—that inborn skills are what separate the best from the rest. You may be more talented than everyone in the room, but that doesn't mean you will be more successful than those sitting around you. In fact, the opposite may prove confoundingly true. You will know people who are clearly less talented who are undeniably more successful. Or you'll experience it in the contrast.

Over the years, I've had the opportunity to invest in professional athletes as a speaker and mindset coach. One of the most difficult challenges in this work is convincing a person with world-class talent that their character is more essential to their success than their natural attributes. Everyone knows in theory that hard work and discipline are important, but how about integrity and humility? In a profession where you're surrounded by the most physically gifted people on earth, all of them playing a game that involves running, catching, blocking, and tackling, you could understand why someone would think character plays a lesser role in their success.

Years ago, I spoke at an event with around five hundred professional football players, which led to me visiting Oakland for a Monday Night Football game. It was the classic rivalry between the Oakland Raiders and the Denver Broncos, and it also happened to be my first time watching JaMarcus Russell play quarterback. Russell was an extraordinary physical specimen. He stood six-foot-six and weighed somewhere north of 260 pounds, but even at that size he was clocked running a 4.7-second forty-yard dash with a vertical leap of thirty-one inches. He had just left LSU, where he won a national championship. Russell's arm strength and raw athleticism made it impossible for the Raiders to pass up on drafting him with the very first pick in the first round. He had both the dimensions and the credentials to be taken number one.

Before I tell you what I saw during the game, let me tell you what stood out to me afterward. The Raiders lost, and I watched Russell leave the stadium with his entourage, seemingly unaffected by another loss. The final score of that game was painfully lopsided. Broncos 41, Raiders 14—the first loss in a season that would end with eleven of them. I certainly did not know the inner workings of what was going on in Russell's life, but my brief observation gave me a sense that he was emotionally detached from the outcome of the game. Which, by the way, is what had translated to the field. He threw more interceptions than touchdowns—which was easy in a way, since there were no touchdowns thrown. Later that season, the performance would be matched by a game with three fumbles, zero touchdowns, and only sixty yards gained through the air.

JaMarcus Russell was born for greatness. He was a singular, once-in-a-lifetime talent. But nowadays, Russell is considered one of the greatest busts in the history of professional football. Did the experts completely misjudge his potential? Did his failure to succeed negate all of the factors that led the Raiders to take him with the first pick? Not at all. Regardless of the complete collapse of his professional football career, every assessment of his talent was accurate and valid.

The problem, of course, is that talent is a hallucinogen. It distorts reality.

In hindsight we can see that JaMarcus Russell was missing the critical ingredients for sustained success. The first clue emerged during his rookie season, when he refused to participate in training camp in an effort to maximize his rookie contract. He missed a crucial window of development, which would have prepared him for the challenge of becoming a professional quarterback. Even when he returned, teammates noted his lack of effort in practice, which delayed the team's ability to play him during the season. A few games in, one of the coaches gave Russell a game tape to study at home, knowing that he never watched the films or put in the work. The following day, Russell returned talking about the plays on the tape, never knowing that the tape was completely blank.

Russell had taken the drug. He convinced himself that his talent was enough. Lesser athletes needed to put in the work, but Russell acted as though he was exempt from such expectations.

It doesn't matter if you're a first-round draft pick or a fast-rising executive. All the talent in the world is not a guarantee of success. At best, talent is a sign of promise. But without discipline, it will never realize its full potential. I cannot say this enough times. For talent to translate into success, it must be forged in the pressure cooker of adversity and centered by character. No matter how talented you are, you will eventually come to the end of your talent. When you come to the end of your talent, you discover the depth of your character.

Years ago, I wrote that if you live long enough, your hard work will be mistaken for talent, and your resilience will be mistaken for genius. I have only become more convinced of this truth since then. It only takes a drop of genius to create something extraordinary. Talent needs you to believe that talent isn't enough. Your real talent—your real greatness—can only be discovered when you start acting as if you must compensate for your deficit of talent with hard work.

The best thing that can happen to a person with extraordinary talent is to somehow be completely unaware of it. If you lean exclusively on your talent, you will collapse under the weight of expectation. In fact, talent can become a liability in that regard. When a person perceives himself to be more talented than everyone else, he struggles to cope when facing setbacks or unexpected challenges. This self-perception can make that person very dangerous. When things go wrong, they are quick to blame other team members or outside factors as the cause. They deflect responsibility, in no small part because they are more psychologically fragile. They believe they are better than everyone else, and they need to ensure that their surroundings confirm this bias. The result is that they play it safe. They only take risks where they are guaranteed to succeed. They have an extraordinarily high self-image with an unexpectedly low level of resilience.

If this is where you find yourself, the first step is to learn how to appreciate other people and to take personal responsibility for failure. If you believe everyone on your team is incompetent, I can assure you that they are not the problem.

The contrast to this is the person who assumes they are less talented than others, who compensates by taking ownership and putting in extraordinary effort. They will knock on a thousand doors risking rejection to make a sale. They will start a company from scratch, since they lack the obvious markers of success that companies look for in a hire. They are willing to move into a new and unknown enterprise, making up for experience with hard work. They are not afraid of failure because failure is not devastating to their psychological well-being. They expect to fail. They also know that failure is not the end of the story, but instead is their pathway to success. This psychological posture makes them more inherently resilient. While they may not feel destined for greatness, they are nonetheless determined to achieve it.

At sixteen years old, I was convinced that I had no talent. I was drowning in self-doubt and constantly underestimating what I was capable of or could accomplish. There was always a voice in the back of my head asking, Why would anyone choose me?

Ironically, I used my sense of inadequacy to my advantage. I decided that since I wasn't qualified and would most likely fail, I might as well dedicate my life to doing the impossible. If I could go back and talk to my teenage self, I would tell him, "You have all the talent you need to live the most extraordinary life you could ever imagine. The question is, will you have the character to sustain it?"

Don't be discouraged if your talent doesn't explode into the world like fireworks. Most of us are late bloomers, possessing latent talent that requires a slow burn. I would always tell my son that if you don't have an obvious talent, then you have the gift of leadership. Your path to success will be character, emotional intelligence, and resilience.

Let your deficit of talent be your fuel, but never allow yourself to have a deficit of character. Aspire for a life of virtue. Be humble. Be kind. Be generous. Be courageous. Have integrity. Tell the truth. Express gratitude. Make love your motive always. Serve. Let who you are be your best feature.

Talent moves fast and burns like a high-octane fuel. Character, on the other hand, prepares you for the long journey ahead. Becoming the number one draft pick is overrated. It's way better to finish first. It's even more important to finish well.

Talent is a hallucinogen. Character keeps it real.

MIND SHIFT #7:

No One Knows
What They Are Doing

One of my friends started a business with his wife and sold it a decade later for just over a billion dollars. This friend is one smart guy, one of the only people I've met who has street smarts *and* a formal Ivy League education. He knows everything about everything. You can pick any topic—economics, politics, graphic novels, mixed martial arts, World Cup soccer, global pandemics—and he will be an expert.

Which is why, when I asked about the process he and his wife used to build their company, his response surprised me. He told me that people keep asking him what strategy they followed, or what their plan looked like at the beginning. "We didn't have a plan," he explained. "We had no idea what it would look like. We had to roll

77

with the punches, and most of the punches came from unexpected directions."

I was shocked. If anyone had all the knowledge required for success, it would be this man. But his memory was, quite simply, "We had no idea what we were doing."

I couldn't believe it. I thought I was the only one.

Every time I start something, I don't just feel like a novice; I feel like an impostor. Here I am, starting a new business or cause, and I have no idea what I'm doing. Who do I think I am, trying to take this on? From where I'm standing, it looks like everyone else knows what they're doing, and I am a pool of ignorance. This is how I feel every time I take on a new challenge.

Every decade of my life I have begun a new venture or launched a new phase of my career. The challenge has been that each new endeavor required an entirely new set of competencies. When I wrote a graphic novel, I had to learn an entirely new structure to writing. All of a sudden, I was figuring out how to develop characters and learning to write narrative arcs. When I dove back into fashion after working as a designer decades earlier, I had to learn fabrics, pattern development, and colorways, while also studying how trends take off and how different areas of culture influence design. When I launched my course, The Art of Communication, and began building a company focused on coaching entrepreneurs to reach optimal performance, the task felt so much bigger than me. The risk was huge and the potential for failure real. I couldn't do it halfway. It was all in or all out.

In each of these scenarios, I had to fight the psychological weight of feeling like a poser. What in the world made me think I could do this? I went all in, even though I had a cacophony of voices in my head telling me I was out of my league, out of my mind.

And yet, nearly every breakthrough in my career has come from deciding not to let my lack of experience or expertise stop me from creating.

The truth is, no matter what direction you choose for your life, on the first day, you are not qualified to do that job. But that does not make you an impostor. It simply makes you a beginner. It's what you do after you start that matters. Well, let me take it back one step: What matters most *is that you start*. You will have a thousand reasons not to launch your new endeavor, and 999 of them will be true. What you must come to grips with is that none of that matters. Eventually, you just have to hit the gas and learn as you go.

As I look back on these past decades for which I'm incredibly grateful, I've had the opportunity to do so many unbelievable things. I've worked as a futurist and senior scientist. I've worked as a documentary filmmaker and an actor. I've worked as an author and writer. I've worked as a fashion designer. I've worked as a peak performance business coach.

I've worked as a carpenter and landscaper and librarian. I've worked as a mindset coach for athletes and as a strategist for entrepreneurs. I've hosted a TV show—actually, two of them. I've worked for multiple universities, developing their master's and doctoral programs. I work with world-class speakers through The Art of Communication and top entrepreneurs through my latest venture, McManus Mastermind.

My early days as a designer were nothing like what I do today. All I knew when I started was what I liked and what I loved to wear. I also had a lot of ideas about where fashion was headed. I knew nothing about fabrics; I just knew what felt good when you put it on. I had to learn the entire design, production, and sales process from scratch.

When I first began working as a director, I was overwhelmed by all the moving parts involved in making a film. You have to orchestrate the location, lighting, sound, camera movements, blocking, script—and, of course, the actors' performances. I wanted everything to be beautiful, so the cinematography had to be world class. I wanted the performances to be authentic and compelling, so I had to learn how to work with actors who were both talented and temperamental. I also needed to know every character in-depth so I could envision how each of them fit into the story as I wanted to tell it.

The first time I ever acted, I was asked to play an assassin for a friend's TV pilot. That friend, who has since gone on to great success as a writer, told me that he'd written the script with me in mind. I wasn't sure how to take the fact that my friend thought of me when creating a character who made his living as an assassin. Not only had I never acted in my life, the character would have to do a number of other things outside my skill set. I needed to learn how to shoot a gun, so we found a former government special agent who was willing to train me. My character would be thrown out of a skyscraper window in another scene, so a friend who built his career as a stunt double on films like *Disturbia* and *Indiana Jones* coached me on how to jump, fall, and land without injuring myself. Oh, and I had to learn how to act, which is not as easy as it looks (and it does not look easy).

From the script, I knew that I would be thrown through skyscraper glass head first. When they described the scene to me, I assumed we would use a material that only looked like glass. Surely that would be dramatically safer. But they explained to me that a substitute would not create the effect needed for the scene. It had to be a real window. In fact, the glass was so thick, the crew had to place explosives on every corner of the pane for it to break properly as I was being thrown through it.

I wasn't ready for any of this, but I am so glad that I didn't wait until I was ready. The one thing I had going for me was that I knew I didn't know what I was doing. They couldn't have found a more teachable person. I was looking in every direction for anyone who could teach me about what I was preparing to attempt. Acting coaches. Stuntmen. Anyone involved in the shoot. There is something absolutely exhilarating about being a beginner, about being an amateur. You have nowhere to go but up. On that first day, you know less than you will ever know. That by itself should give you a lot of confidence.

The one effort I haven't listed in this chapter is my life's work of being a pastor at Mosaic. That's because I don't see pastoring as a job. Starting Mosaic and serving there over the last thirty years has been a calling, a passion, and a privilege, not an occupation. Still, I would say that starting Mosaic was the greatest entrepreneurial risk of my life—and the most satisfying one.

When you're starting something from scratch, the bad news is that if you feel you have no idea what you're doing, that feeling is pretty spot-on. The good news is you're exactly where everyone else is when they start something new. The spectrum doesn't range from the person who knows everything to the person who doesn't know anything. The spectrum is the person who thinks they know everything they need to know, versus the person who works tirelessly to fill in the gaps.

The ironic thing is that the person who has absolute certainty that they know everything is in a more dangerous position than a novice. When you are living with the delusion that you know everything needed in order to succeed, you have a huge blind spot, and you are less likely to learn the skills and knowledge that are crucial for your success. When you know you don't know, you are perfectly postured for learning.

Sometimes it will appear as if you're the only person who doesn't know what they are doing. You will do your best to hide your sense of inadequacy and hope no one finds you out as an impostor.

There will be those who have so much more confidence than you. That doesn't mean they actually know more than you. And yes, there will be those who do know more than you and are better at what they do. The key, though, is that they started just like you.

When they started, they had no idea what they were doing. But they did it anyway.

Do it wrong.

Do it bad.

Do it raw.

Keep doing it until you know what you're doing.

Just never stop learning and growing.

Let what you don't know be your competitive advantage.

When the critics get into your head, make the mind shift: No one knows what they are doing.

And neither do you.

MIND SHIFT #8:

Bitterness, and Other Poisons That Will Kill You

Living in Los Angeles can distort your sense of reality. The Harvard School of Public Health projects that close to half the U.S. population will struggle with obesity by 2030. It goes on to tell us that currently 40 percent of American adults have obesity and 18 percent have severe obesity. This research is published in the *New England Journal of Medicine*. You would never know that living here in Southern California. This is the land of 7 percent body fat, washboard stomachs, and beach bodies. I don't know the statistics, but I imagine that we also have a disproportionate number of gyms, health clubs, and personal trainers. The level of commitment to physical health on the West Coast is really quite impressive, even if it is motivated by vanity.

I recently subjected myself to something called a

DEXA scan. It tells you the exact amount and location of the muscle mass and fat throughout your body. People use it to determine where they need to lose fat and gain muscle for optimal health. There's no need to go into detail about what I discovered, but I will say it wasn't pretty.

From a physical perspective, Angelenos are committed to getting rid of all the extra baggage. But in thirty years of living here, I've found that the commitment doesn't always carry over to their emotional well-being. I've counseled hundreds if not thousands of people, and the lingering effect of past hurts and wounds is by far the most debilitating issue I've found. People describe feeling bitter toward their parents, their significant others, former co-workers, even people who haven't been in their lives for years. Frankly, one of the hardest people to help is a bitter person. When someone is discouraged, you can call out their strengths and tell them all the ways you admire them. When someone is grieving, you can love them and be present in their grief. But when someone is bitter, they are rarely open to the process required to find healing. They see forgiveness as a weakness. They don't want to concede anything to the person who offended or hurt them. It dominates their thoughts to the point where it's impossible to think about anything else.

One of the safest predictions I can make is that all of us will be hurt, wounded, or even betrayed by someone who was once close to us. In fact, betrayal can only happen when it's someone you trust. There may be no human experience more difficult to overcome than feeling betrayed by someone you love.

Sadly, for many people this happens early in life. It's hard to explain divorce to an eight-year-old. It's hard to explain to a child who suffered abuse that there are people in the world you can trust. It's hard to explain to someone who believed the words "I love you" that not every man will leave you when you need him most. These woundings live on in our subconscious, and they become a part of the story we believe about ourselves. You may not remember the trauma, but it has left you traumatized. You were too young to remember when you were powerless, but the feeling of being powerless is still with you, and you've sworn that no one will ever make you feel that way again.

We know that obesity or a bad diet can lead to heart disease. But bitterness, too, is a silent killer. Nothing will steal your health, your relationships, your joy faster than carrying your emotional baggage with you. Bitterness, resentment, envy, and unforgiveness can poison your soul and cost you the intimacy of being loved and truly known.

Humans are a multidimensional species. We live in the past, present, and future all at the same time. We live in the past through our memories. We live in the future through our dreams. We live in the present through our choices. When the three are integrated, we live at our optimal level of health and wholeness. The future pulls us forward. The present keeps us grounded. The past calls us backward.

It is fascinating from a psychological perspective that two people can have virtually the same traumatic experience and come out of it completely different. One response can leave us broken; another can create internal structures for success. Either way, our experiences are not the defining ingredient in our lives. It is our response to those experiences—how we remember them and interpret them—that shapes who we become.

Over the past three decades, you and I have been given access to a global incubator that allows us to study human behavior in real time. It is called the internet. What we've learned about human behavior is that we are far more attracted to the negative than to the positive. Negative news about a celebrity will travel far faster than positive news. People are more likely to respond when they see a negative comment than they are when they see a positive one. In particular, I am amazed at how relentlessly cruel people can be on social media after a breakup. There is perhaps nothing more dangerous to your reputation than to have an ex who loves social media.

Some blame the internet for this obsession with negativity, but I've come to believe that what we are seeing through social media is the external reflection of our own internal worlds. Even offline, negative emotions seem to stay with us longer than positive emotions. The euphoria of a positive experience, no matter how intense or exhilarating, will last for only a moment. Negative emotions, on the other hand, have a long tail and are far more difficult to overcome. We must choose positive emotions, while negative emotions seem to choose us.

That's why optimism is a discipline. It takes discipline to see the good when things are going bad. It takes discipline to see beauty in the midst of tragedy. It takes discipline to see the best in people when they let us down. It takes discipline to forgive when the person does not deserve it. It takes discipline to reject the negative voices in our heads and choose to listen to the optimist who's cheering us on.

Bitterness is a poison that numbs you before it kills you. Without the bitterness, all you will feel is the pain of the lost job opportunity, the broken relationship, the loved one who let you down. When you can't take that level of pain anymore, you harden your heart with bitterness. In theory, you're protecting your heart from being hurt again. But bitterness doesn't protect your heart, it hardens it. When you are bitter, that becomes the only emotion you can feel.

What's worse is that bitterness cannot be contained. When you hold on to bitterness against one person, you become bitter against the entire world. You carry bitterness into every new relationship. You become slow to trust. You keep your heart guarded. You get angry at the slightest provocation. You can't explain why you're so easily offended, or why you always feel a sense of betrayal.

The reality is that when you are bitter, you are no longer in your own story. Your thoughts, actions, and other relationships are being poisoned by what happened with someone else. You unwittingly become a prisoner in the story of the one who hurt you, disappointed you, or betrayed you.

To be free, you need a mind shift.

The only thing that frees us from bitterness is the one thing we do not want to do. We don't want to forgive. That's letting the other person off the hook. Why would we ever do that? Besides, maybe they didn't even ask for forgiveness. Can you really forgive someone who doesn't even feel they need it? Just the thought of having to forgive someone who hurt you in the past can make you feel angry all over again.

But bitterness is not an emotion you are designed to carry. Bitterness is your soul's way of letting you know that you are out of alignment. It is your soul screaming to be set free from a negative emotion it was never intended to hold.

Every problem you will ever face will ultimately boil down to people. It would be a perfect world if it were not for people. People will always be the problem—and they will always be the solution. You are not exempt from this dilemma. You and I are both the problem and the solution. It's why the most important skill you will ever learn is to forgive.

Pause for a moment and think about the people who might need forgiveness from you. Is it time to forgive your parents? Is it time to forgive your spouse? Is it time to forgive your ex? Is it time to forgive your boss? Is it time to forgive your former business partner? Is it time to forgive yourself?

One of the most curious things about human emotions is that an emotion cannot exist without a story. This may be the fundamental reason why we have dreams and nightmares. When our subconscious is dealing with an unresolved emotion, it creates a story to give that emotion a place to live. If it's a negative emotion, our brain internalizes it as a nightmare. If we are brimming over with positive emotions such as hope, or love, or joy, our brains play out those emotions in a story we call a dream.

Just like our dreams and nightmares, the emotions we're carrying from the past can only be sustained within the stories we tell ourselves. Hopefully your inner narrative is a positive one. I'm built for this challenge; I've faced failure before and overcame it, so I can do it again; I love when people underestimate me and I get to prove them wrong; I am unstoppable; I am worthy of love; My pain didn't break me, it just made me stronger; I was put on this earth to accomplish something extraordinary.

If you want to be free of negative emotions, you must

write a new story. This begins by taking control over the story that is defining you. Identify the experiences that have shaped you, the memories that haunt you. Don't try to forget them. Instead, turn them into fuel. You are not a powerless victim, no matter what you have been through. Refuse to let anyone or anything have that kind of control over your life. Your pain is real, but the feeling of powerlessness is a lie. It wasn't your choice that pain became a part of your story, and you cannot be free of it if you ignore it and pretend it didn't happen to you. But the trauma is not who you are.

You are a part of a bigger story. Yours is a story of hope. Yours is a story of resilience. Yours is a story of faith, of challenges overcome. You have wounds, but they are not your story. Your story is the story of healing. Refuse to allow the negative moments of your life to define who you will become. What the mind shift allows you to see is that bitterness is a poison and forgiveness is the cure.

To understand forgiveness as a strength is one of the most powerful mind shifts you will ever make. Forgiveness is not an emotion. Forgiveness is an art form. It is the most elegant expression of love. Forgiveness requires a level of mastery that very few ever attain. It is the highest level of thinking when it comes to human relationships and the health of your own soul, and it's the only way to keep your negative experiences from writing the story of who you become.

You Find What You Are

Have you ever wondered how it's possible that you are surrounded by so many incompetent people? We are about to solve that problem.

By contrast, have you ever been overwhelmed by how many amazing people are in your life? If so, you are going to love this chapter.

If you're single, you've probably heard the advice that if you want to find the right person, you need to *become* the right person. What they didn't tell you is that this rule doesn't apply only to dating. It's a universal principle. The world has eight billion people in it. Each one is unique and different and also similar.

I've learned that relationships work like a moth to flames. If you are compassionate, you will find compassionate people all over the world. If you love adventure, you will find adventurous people everywhere you go. If you are trustworthy, you will find a world full of trustworthy people. If you are hopeful, you will find people full of hope all around you. The world is full of people just like you. But know that you will not find what you are looking for; you will find what you are.

At this point in my life, I've been to more than seventy countries across the world. Travel is one of my greatest joys, and I am so grateful for the privilege of making it part of my work. I have never spent time in a country I did not enjoy. Every place I've ever visited has been unique and extraordinary in some way. I must confess, though, I remember some countries better than others.

In hindsight, I can see that my clearest memories are not about where they happened but who they happened with. I'll never forget slipping across the Lebanese border into Syria to visit the city of Damascus, shortly before 9/11. At the time, Damascus was known as the epicenter of terrorism, and if I remember correctly, it boasted the highest population of professional assassins in the world. Walking down streets that had been written about for thousands of years was surreal. Another highlight was shopping throughout the street markets, bartering over a leather jacket.

What I remember the most, though, are three men I met on that trip. The first man looked like he was in his late twenties. He saw our group walking down the street, and for whatever reason he chose to walk directly toward me with a smile on his face. "Do you speak English?" he asked in a hopeful tone. I nodded and said, "Yes, I do." He responded eagerly, "Wonderful, wonderful. I love speaking English. You come to my house, and have dinner with me and my family. We can speak English all night together." Our schedule did not allow for that to happen. Still, that encounter made my entire trip. I could never again see Damascus the way it had been described to me before. People told me it was the most dangerous city in the world. Friends cautioned that it was unsafe, especially for Westerners, to walk freely about the city. But when I think about Damascus now, all I can see is an incredibly kind young Muslim man who invited me to come to his home and share a meal.

Another person I will never forget from Damascus was the man whose home we actually did visit. He hosted me and my friends and served us a banquet fit for kings. His kindness was palpable. He was genuinely interested in us and endlessly curious about our lives. He treated us as honored guests, and we left feeling like family.

The third person who marked my trip to Damascus was a man who owned a leather store on the ancient streets of this historic city. The leather shops in that market were endless, but his store stood out mostly because of him. He was charismatic, sharp-witted, and hilarious. I liked him right away and knew I had to buy something from him. It was so much fun negotiating with him. I had been instructed earlier that it was very important that

I appear to have lost the negotiation. The men and women who work the street markets are very proud of their skills. It was equally as important that I put up a fight. Don't buy too quickly. Don't walk away too abruptly. Leave room for the conversation to continue. It was like a dance.

I have only fond memories of Damascus, and this has been true for me all over the world. Everywhere I go, I find good, kind, beautiful people who reinforce my view of humanity. Even when I've entered places considered hostile to outsiders, such as Medellín, Islamabad, Bogotá, Baalbek, Phnom Penh, San Salvador, Paris, or Los Angeles, I've always been pleasantly surprised. It's not that I am blind to the human condition. I'm not naïve to the darkness that can dwell within each of us. I fully understand that what each of us needs most is the transformation of our heart. Still, this does not diminish my unrelenting optimism toward humanity. Look for the best in people, and you will find it.

But the opposite is also true. Going back to the earlier example, the reason you can't meet the right person until you're the right person is that you're stuck on the wrong frequency. For every practical concern, the person you're looking for does not exist—at least, they do not exist to you. You will dismiss them or discount them, because they do not resonate with who you are and what you are actually looking for in a partner, a colleague, or a friend. That's why people keep dating different versions of the same person even when they say they want someone different. If you have become convinced that everyone is the same, it's because *you* are still the same. If you want to upgrade the kind of people in your life, you need to upgrade *your* life.

One of the advantages of serving the same community for more than thirty years is that you get to counsel people at different life stages and watch them develop. The optimist in me would say that I have seen people make dramatic changes in their lives—which is true. The realist in me would add that most people don't change—which is also true. Too often, people stay at a singular frequency, or stage of development, for most of their adulthood.

The person living at the highest frequency is someone who has both achieved great personal success and committed themselves to living a genuinely humanitarian life. Their level of sacrifice and commitment to serve others is always inspiring. When I'm coaching someone who lives at this frequency, my work is about helping them gain greater clarity, maximize their impact, and maintain the health of their inner world.

One of the more common frequencies is the person who is struggling to find their life purpose. I've met countless twenty-year-olds here in LA who are trying to find themselves without taking the risks necessary to test their own potential. I've also seen too many people in their thirties and forties who are still acting like they're in their twenties. Their narrative is: Once I'm healed, I can help; Once I've found myself, then I can serve others. It's almost as if they hope their destiny will find them on its own.

These are by far the most difficult conversations. It is exhausting trying to convince a person that they need to work on themselves. It is also challenging to convince a person that empathy is not about denial. Genuine empathy moves you to accept responsibility for the problems you are facing in life. Often, the most empathetic thing you can do for another person is to tell them the truth in love.

At one of my Mastermind events, an entrepreneur with thirty employees asked for my advice on creating a culture where his best producers would stay with him instead of leaving for competitors. He had recently lost his top two producers, and he was concerned he might lose more. At the same time, he described his team as the reason his organization was not thriving. When I asked him to paint a picture of the company's culture, he proceeded to tell me everything that was wrong with the thirty people who worked for him.

I took him through two brief exercises. I asked him to list at least five positive things about himself. He did it quickly and easily. Then I asked him to choose any of his thirty employees and tell me any positive attributes about them. Brain freeze. He literally could not think of one positive characteristic for a single person on his team. As we dug deeper, we were able to see what was really happening.

This man was struggling with the massive psychological tension we discussed in the chapter about talent. His company was failing, but he believed he was too gifted to fail. So there was only one clear explanation: His team was incompetent. I gave the man some homework. I told him that in the upcoming week I wanted him to begin to identify three positive traits for each person who worked for him. He told me that it would be very hard, but I assured him he was up to the task. The story is unfolding even as I write. Let's hope he gains new eyes to see his team's greatness.

The best assessment of who you are is not who you say you are, but who you are convinced others are. If you perceive people as needing to be told what to do, it's because you need to be told what to do. If you perceive others as needing praise and affirmation, it's because you need praise and affirmation. If you perceive others as needing a great deal of time to make a decision, it is because you need a great deal of time to make decisions. We do not see the world as it is. We see the world as we are.

Be wary when someone talks to you only about what is wrong in the world. Their perspective might tell you less about the world than it does about the condition of their own soul. When a politician is always preaching against the rich, you might want to check their hidden accounts. When they are always preaching about moral decline, don't be shocked if you later discover their immorality. When they call every other politician a liar, you can be pretty sure they are lying to you. We unconsciously bring light to our own shadows. If you choose to fill your soul with faith and hope, laughter and love, your journey will lead you to a beautiful world and a beautiful life.

Here is the mind shift: You will find in the world what you bring to the world. Stop expecting people to be different until you are different. Don't expect to find better people until you are committed to becoming a better person. Change the world within you, and that will change the world around you. In fact, the opposite works just as powerfully. Change what you believe about people, and it will change the people who are drawn to you.

Love has a frequency. Hope has a frequency. Faith has a frequency. Courage has a frequency. Integrity has a frequency. Compassion has a frequency. Generosity has a frequency. When you choose to live in these frequencies, you are drawn to those who are like-minded, and they are drawn to you.

I confess that I leverage my life in a very particular direction. I am convinced that every human being is created in the image of God and that, even when we're most broken, there always remains a reflection of that reality. So I search for the good in people. I search for that part of them that reflects the best part of being human. Sometimes you have to look harder to find it, but I know that divine spark is in there somewhere.

I am convinced we are designed to live a life defined by love, and hope, and, yes, even faith. I am far from living in a way that reflects these ideals fully, but I am genuine in my desire to be the best expression of myself. Those are the kind of people I see everywhere.

The world is full of amazing people, living life like a great adventure. I want to be able to see them. I am committed to living at that frequency, and I am convinced we have more that would bring us together than would tear us apart. I have yet to discover a country, a workplace, or a community where wonderful, fascinating, and welcoming people weren't waiting there for me. If I have one regret, it is that I do not have time enough to know them all.

MIND SHIFT #10:

Be Average
(At Almost Everything)

Have I mentioned that the American educational system is completely broken? I don't say that as an indictment of public education. I've traveled the world, and I am very grateful for the effort over the years to make education available to every child in every place across the United States.

Still, there are good arguments that our current system of education is obsolete. We are no longer a world leader in basic skills such as reading, writing, and mathematics. There are also serious concerns about what materials are being selected and how those materials are chosen for educating our children. While these are all critical issues to be discussed when we consider education reform, I'm talking about something far more fundamental.

How many of us remember the content of what we learned from first through twelfth grades? How many of us sat through subjects that have since proven to have absolutely no relevance to our effectiveness in our chosen professions? Have you ever secured that promotion or met a longtime goal and thought to yourself, *Oh! That's why I needed to learn the periodic table!*

What we need during those years is one basic skill: We need to learn how to learn. If you learned how to learn, you will have left school prepared for every challenge ahead. The problem is that learning how to do algebra doesn't teach you the kind of learning that you'll do in real life. The system pounds into our subconscious: Repeat after me; Fill in the blank; We have the answers, so you just memorize them and write them down. If you live this way as an adult, you will spend your days fulfilling someone else's agenda, never tapping into your unique potential.

Our school system is built on the fusing of two educational philosophies. The first is the British educational system, which enshrines standardization and conformity as the best approaches for training undisciplined minds. The goal is to teach every student the same skills across a wide variety of disciplines. From first through twelfth grades, you are being trained to be an employee. Obedience is valued over creativity. Then you go to college. If you happen to have any entrepreneurial instincts, education will do the best it can to squeeze them out of you.

The second guiding value is the concept of the Renaissance man. Leon Battista Alberti advocated for the notion that "a man can do all things if he will." Alberti lived in Italy during the fifteenth century, a time when people idealized the "universal man": an intellectual philosopher who would gain mastery of the sciences, the arts, and the humanities.

This is why a college degree takes four years today. They want you to be well-rounded, so you end up taking geology and wasting precious hours of your life studying rocks. Don't get me wrong: If you went through the school system without learning how to read, write, and count, the school system failed you. I also believe everyone should have a second language, but find it absurd that we wait so long to introduce it in high school and college, when students' brains have already rigidified and diminished in the natural flexibility needed to learn new languages. We should be teaching a second language in elementary school, one that the students will most practically need throughout their lives.

But here's the real problem. When the system tells us we're supposed to be good at everything, education becomes all about dabbling. We learn a little bit about everything and much about nothing. If the original concept was to make everyone great at everything, we have done the opposite—we've made everyone average at everything. Instead of pressuring people to make straight A's, maybe we should have been helping them find their one

A in an ocean of C's. Maybe the first eighteen years of our lives would have been better spent learning to be average at almost everything—except your one thing.

Truth be told, I was a terrible student. I just wasn't that interested in the subjects that they made me sit through. When I finished high school at age seventeen, I felt as though the label "failure" was already written on my tomb.

But the moment I left school, it was like the rules of the game completely changed. It was no longer about who could achieve while sitting behind a desk in the safety of a classroom. Now it was about who could survive the streets and create a future out of nothing. Gone was the emphasis on memorizing material. It was about who could adapt to change and capitalize on uncertainty. Learning was now a matter of life and death. Learning would now be the difference between eating and not eating. My ability to learn would determine whether I would have a roof over my head. It was no longer about knowing a little bit about everything. Now it was all about learning what I needed to know to create the life I wanted to live.

It's amazing how teachable I suddenly became when the implications of my learning were clear. Every day was a final exam. Did I solve the problem? Did I gain the skills to get the job done? Did I earn the customer's trust and get the contract? Was I compelling enough to move the audience? Did I solve the financial crisis and meet our organization's budget? Did my mentoring make the leaders more effective? Did my investment transform their corporate culture? Did I help the company who contracted me scale and surpass their goals? Did I learn what I needed to learn to accomplish what I needed to accomplish? No longer did I have to be good at everything. I just had to believe I was created to be good at *something*. My job was to find that something and build on it.

When we spend so much time trying to be good at everything, it costs us precious time that could be spent becoming great at what we're designed to do. When you care about something, it becomes a filter by which you sift out everything else that demands your time. No one is capable of meaningful engagement with every issue, problem, or skill.

Just ask Michael Jordan, who was the greatest basketball player to ever step on the court—and a major disappointment as a professional baseball player. I think it could be argued that Jordan had the talent to become a great baseball player. He simply did not make the time. There is one simple reason for that: You cannot be great at everything. You have a finite amount of energy and time on this earth, and you must choose how to use it. If you choose to be a jack-of-all-trades, you will be a master of none.

I have had the privilege of working closely with individuals who knew their life mission, had a ruthless sense of focus, and felt no need to care about everything. They directed their compassion and concern like valuable resources. They gave themselves permission to be average at everything else except their one thing. With their one thing, they were determined to bring their best.

Erin Rank cares about one thing: helping deserving families buy homes they could never afford on their own. Her singular focus makes her the perfect person to lead Habitat for Humanity here in Los Angeles, where the organization has raised hundreds of millions of dollars and helped over five hundred families become home-owners.

Scott Harrison is convinced that water is everything. Years ago, Scott founded a nonprofit called charity: water. There can be no ambiguity about what he or his organiza-tion is about. His life mission has been to tell the story of how we can change the world when everyone has access to clean water. Recently he sent me an encouraging text letting me know that the organization he founded to pro-vide clean water mostly in Africa was now raising over $125 million a year. Of course, after he finished his text, he sent me the emoji of a water drop.

Tiyanjane Dzilankhulani is passionate about one thing above all others: helping young girls raised in the bush of Malawi receive an education and a future. Tia believes the girls deserve every opportunity that is made available for boys. She believes she can break the cycle of young girls becoming child brides and living trapped in desperate poverty. She is the founder of an organization called Girl Shine, which operates a school for girls in the country. Tia is changing Malawi one young woman at a time, one life at a time, one future at a time.

My wife, Kim, has been involved in Malawi for the past seven years, and Tia's work has become very important to her. They act like sisters and actually have very similar personalities. I recently joined Kim on one of her projects, and I can tell you there are a lot of needs in the region. Is it wrong, then, that Tia's organization doesn't fight food insecurity, or create opportunities for boys? Of course not. Her singular focus allows her to do what she does better than anyone else. She knows she can't solve all the nation's problems, but she can invest in the girls who attend her school and make sure they have a chance to shine.

When I look back on my life, I see that there were seasons when I tried to do too many things. I genuinely cared about more initiatives than I could give my time, energy, and life to. Narrowing my focus has been one of the most necessary and painful decisions I've had to make. For example, I love LA and have chosen to plant my life here. When I made that decision thirty years ago, I felt a calling to this city. I also felt a deep connection to New York, Paris, and Tokyo. I felt torn when I said yes to Los Angeles because I was also saying no to those other extraordinary cities.

The same goes for my career path. I love everything about making movies. I love acting, and directing, and writing screenplays. If I had another life, maybe I would have gone into the film industry. But I have only one life, and I had to choose where I would spend it.

I've come to realize that the "yes" is so much easier than the "no." But you cannot do everything. So choose your something well. The "no" is as much a part of your calling as the "yes." I'm average at almost everything. I'm good with that. The average in my life is not who I am. It is who I am not.

Liberate yourself from the tyranny of obligation. It's not all on you. You do not have the capacity to do something about everything. It doesn't mean that other things aren't important to you. They're just not your responsibility, your calling, or your mission in life. The sooner you can make peace with this, the faster you will move forward in your life.

Most likely, you will have people in your life who are passionate about things you're simply not passionate about. It doesn't make their mission less valuable because it is not yours. Everyone has a role to play in the good that needs to be done in the world. Find yours and give it everything you have.

This will be true in every arena of your life. If you're great at math, keep going. If you're not great at math, hire a good accountant. Be good at something, but with the same level of intention, choose to be average at a lot of things. In fact, be average at almost everything. Stop wasting your energy where it does not belong. Be great at being you. The sooner you give yourself permission to live an intentional life, the more unstoppable you will become.

Leave the Renaissance man back in the Renaissance. Know what you're about. Know what matters to you. Know where you are committed to greatness, and make that your life. Get A's in what really matters to you. Don't sweat it if you get B's and C's on everything else. When you find your greatness you make your average irrelevant.

Success Weighs More Than Failure

There are times when I feel like I'm playing a game of last man standing. Most of the high-powered leaders I've known over the last forty years have disappeared from the scene. Some discredited and disqualified themselves from leading their organizations. From infidelity to the abuse of power, from financial impropriety to fraud, from burnout to mental breakdowns, the weight of leadership has caused a great deal of damage in many of their lives. Others are still at the helm of their companies but have lost their marriages, their children, and their families. The weight of success was too heavy a burden to bear.

If life and experience have taught me anything, it's that success weighs more than failure. If you think failure is hard to carry, wait until you have to carry the weight of success. It's easier to be liked when you fail. It's easier for others to empathize with you when you fail. It's easier to have people assume the best of you when you fail. The moment you succeed, everything changes. Success will cost you friends. Success will cost you goodwill. Success will cost you the benefit of the doubt.

We often pursue success, however we define it, in hopes that it will improve our lives. We may also be convinced that wealth is the key to our happiness. But as much as success is a blessing, it can also be a burden. If a wise man prepares for failure, the wiser one prepares for success. If the day comes when you are placed on the throne, will you be able to carry the weight of its responsibility?

For several years I've taught at a Mastermind group where, in order to join, a person's company must be valued at a minimum of one hundred million dollars. I speak at their events several times a year and have ongoing relationships with many of the members. Frankly, before being invited, I never knew that there were communities where people pay six figures to be involved. The room is filled with some of the most driven and interesting people you could ever hope to meet. My relationship with them has evolved from an audience I would speak to, to friends I do life with. I am there for them, and they are there for me. Whenever we need each other, we show up, regardless of whether the crisis is business or personal.

Sometimes I don't know what qualified me for this work. When Kim and I got married, we were poor. For the next five years, I never made more than sixteen thousand dollars annually, and we slept on the floor because we could not afford a bed. Between the two of us, our income still didn't touch the welfare line. But we were so happy, it never occurred to us to think of ourselves as poor. Our lives were so rich. We laughed a lot. We enjoyed our lives. We loved being together. Kim was my wealth, and I think I was hers. We had meaning. We had purpose. We were happy.

Our lives are very different now. We are both incredibly grateful for the success we've experienced over the years. It was unexpected. We are both idealists. We were happy to follow Jesus, serve humanity, and allow our success to be measured through intangible wealth.

Life is much more complicated now. Today, I am responsible for more than a half dozen businesses I have started. I write books. I speak across the world. I lead a Mastermind community. I do in-depth business consulting and elite-level leadership development. I also lead Mosaic, the community of faith I founded.

I love my life. Yet it would be an understatement to say that I feel the weight of all these responsibilities every single day of my life.

Kim has incredible responsibilities too. She travels across the world leading Mosaic Global, the humanitarian arm of our community. She also founded Mosaic Education Initiative, which finds mentors for young refugees and foster youth transitioning out of the system while also helping them qualify for scholarships into college. She has invested the last seven years in a development project in Malawi, culminating in the building of a premier primary school. In addition, she spearheads the transitional services for a group of mostly Muslim refugees here in Los Angeles. She also serves on the board of Habitat for Humanity and is actively involved in building houses across our city.

All this to say, our life is every bit as meaningful now as it was when we were newlyweds. But the weight of that success has made our lives much more complicated. As a public figure, I'm aware that people are rarely trying to dig up the good we do. There is an implicit cultural assumption that if you have financial success, you must have done something unethical to achieve it. And so, if your happiness and sense of self rely on the approval of others, success will crush you.

Every aspect of success carries a price tag. If your aspiration is fame, it will cost you your privacy. If your ambition is power, it may cost you peace of mind. If your desire is self-indulgent pleasures, it will cost you a future. If your goal is wealth, it may cost you your soul. It's not that any of these goals is inherently wrong. It's that while money, fame, and the trappings of success can be extraordinary outcomes of a life well lived, they make for terrible objectives. Your life purpose must be bigger than simply becoming famous, rich, or powerful. If these are the fuel of your life, you will always be running on empty. You will achieve everything you've ever wanted and still feel as if you have nothing. You must live for more. There is no level of success that will give meaning to your life. If you do not already have meaning in your life, all that you attain in life will have no meaning.

I cannot speak to you seriously enough in this moment. I would rather be the voice of caution than remain silent and leave you unprepared.

Shortly before the pandemic, I was asked to come and speak at an event on the East Coast. The host was a young man who had made several billion dollars before the age of forty. I knew the moment I met him that I hadn't been his choice to be the keynote speaker. It didn't require much intuition. He didn't bother to come and greet me before the event, and he ignored me when he walked by me in the conference center. I leaned over to the friend who had secured me the invitation, and he acknowledged that I had been imposed on the host. He only wanted billionaires speaking, and I definitely did not qualify.

But somehow, in the course of the evening, he and I made a connection. His wife, who was also sitting at the table with us, was clearly the love of his life. He and I talked for quite some time. Our conversations traveled a wide galaxy of topics, from human anthropology to the relationship between quantum mechanics and organizational leadership, before getting to more personal things like the elusive nature of happiness. He told me that I reminded him of his wife, that our brains worked in very similar ways. Then he began to express how grateful he was for the meaningful conversation we'd ended up having.

After the event, I was waiting in the lobby for a car to pick me up and take me back to the hotel. The host followed me outside and immediately started to ask me deeply personal questions about his life. I had taken a risk earlier and bluntly told him what I sensed about him: that he was empty, desperate, and hiding his pain behind his possessions. He worked so hard to ensure that everyone would see him the way he wanted to be seen. But I told him that I could see him, and I knew he wasn't well. Beneath the success, he seemed fragile and hopeless.

I can't really explain this without attributing it to God, but for whatever reason, I am able to see inside of people in this way. I don't want to. Too often what I see is pain. And that's what I saw in this highly successful man. I needed him to know that there was not enough money in the world to hide the pain he was carrying in his soul.

Before I even made it back to my hotel, he called me on my cell and the conversation continued. I offered to help him with what he was going through, but he declined. It was just too private and painful. I could tell from everything he said that he was desperate to open up. But in the end, it was more than he felt safe to share. He closed the door. "I've got this!" was pretty much his response. I don't know how many times I've heard that. I told him that even if it wasn't with me, he needed to allow someone into his life to help him find health and whole-ness. I never heard from him again.

A few months later, I read in the paper that he had taken his life. The words of Jesus are penetrating in moments like these: "What does it profit a man to gain the whole world and lose his soul?"

Never forget that when you gain the whole world, it's really heavy. When I studied mythology in the sixth grade, I remember seeing the image of Atlas carrying the entire world on his shoulders. Even the Greeks knew that such weight can only be carried by the gods. Success can crush those who are ill prepared to bear it, especially when success is only defined by *more*. Like a siren song, it woos and calls you, and then it seeks to hold you captive.

You might think that I am against the pursuit of success and against ambition, but the contrary would be true. In fact, I want you to have great ambition. I want you to achieve a ridiculous level of success. If I could be so bold, I hope the advice in this book inspires you to create such extraordinary wealth that you have millions, if not billions, of dollars to give away and invest in those who are doing good across the world. I just don't want you to be blind to what you are working to achieve.

Contrary to what popular wisdom tells us, success will not change you. What success does is give you the freedom and power to become who you really are. You will not become generous when you are rich if you were not generous when you were poor. You will not have integrity when you are in power if you did not have integrity when you were powerless. You will not be humble when you gain fame if you did not have humility when you were anonymous. Success only magnifies what is already within you.

Act like you are going to be successful. Become the best version of you *now*. Spend as much energy developing your character as you do your bank account. Invest in yourself even more than you invest in your net worth. Once you have wealth and fame and power, it will be nearly impossible to find people who will tell you the truth—especially if you lack humility, and kindness, and generosity. You can't afford to take that baggage with you.

They key is that you can't do any of this alone. Surround yourself with people who make you better, who aren't afraid to call you out. Don't just expect loyalty; be loyal. Be kind. Remain teachable. Always be grateful for what you have and be grateful for the people in your life. Keep your word and keep your commitments. Always give more than you take. Measure your success not by how much you make but by how much you give. This is the gritty stuff that gets you ready for the shiny stuff.

They say that money can't buy happiness, but that isn't completely true. What you do with your money can give you immeasurable happiness—just not in the way you would think. If you want your money to make you stupid happy, start giving it away. Some of the most joyful people I know are those who've been generous with their tremendous wealth. Some of the kindest people I know run some of the biggest companies in the world. Some of the humblest people I know have attained incredible fame, and still their favorite place to be is at home with their families.

These people are the material of legends. They build schools for the underprivileged. They build homes for the homeless. They feed the hungry. They bring hope to the hopeless. They create opportunities for others and are determined to create a better future.

Yes, most of them have extraordinary homes. Many of them have yachts and private planes, or more cars than they can drive. They certainly have more than most of us could ever imagine owning. But I decided long ago that instead of envying what others possessed, I would celebrate them. They're exactly the kind of people you would want to have great success. Long before they even knew they could pay the rent, they decided the kind of people they would be, and the kind of lives they would live. They not only understand the weight of success, they understand the stewardship, responsibility, and opportunity it brings. They absolutely enjoy their lives. They earned it. Success doesn't crush them. It doesn't steal their happiness, or their relationships, or their lives.

Their example has taught me that success doesn't have to be a cautionary tale. If you put in the work, you will have the strength to carry the weight of success and finish well.

There Is No Such Thing as Too Much of a Good Thing

If you study the literature on health and wholeness, you will hear about the importance of balance. You will hear from every direction that the key to living well is to give equal time and energy to your work, your marriage, your family, your health, your faith, and of course, your dreams. I understand what people are advocating for when they give this advice. No one would argue that it's a good idea to obsess over your work to the point of neglecting your spouse or your kids. But the problem with the concept of balance is that it often creates a mental construct that everything in your life should be equal. We surrender to the belief that we must mitigate and even restrain every aspect of our lives, even when it's what we are passionate about, the thing that's most life-giving to us.

Not everything in life carries the same weight. Love,

for example, is not balanced. Even if you tried, you would not have the capacity to love everyone at the same level. Love takes you out of balance. When you love someone, they move to the epicenter of your life. Your entire universe is rearranged by the gravitational pull of who they are. In fact, when you come to love someone at the deepest level, you realize that you will never love anyone else in the same way. There is no balance there. Everything is leveraged in a singular direction.

Individuals who are focused on balance tend to end up looking very much the same. They've accepted someone else's definition of what a balanced life looks like, and in that process, they've rounded off the jagged edges of who they are. What began as a search for harmony ends up looking like apathy. It's one of the reasons I've never believed in balance. If anything, the best-lived lives are radically skewed. Passionate people are rarely balanced. There is a fire that burns inside of them, a love for what they do. They always find a way to talk about it, no matter what the conversation. They are convinced everyone should feel the same way. Those without passion might call them obsessed, and they are right. When someone is living out their passions, they feel most alive.

If you are fortunate enough to find a career that you love, you will never fully understand why other people look forward to vacations. You may set aside a week or two to enjoy your family and friends, but it is not because your work is a burden to you. You love your work. Work is not something you have to do, it's something you get to do.

We're often focused on the wrong side of the equation. We don't need balance; we need intention and alignment. We need to spend the first part of our lives figuring out what we love to do, and then the next part of our lives figuring out how to do it.

When you live a life of intention, you not only begin to get rid of things that are not good for you, you get rid of things that are not *for* you. For example, I do not play golf. My stepfather played on a semi-professional level, and I saw how much time it takes to be good at golf. I made a personal decision early on in my life that golf was not worth that level of commitment for me. For a while, I went even further than that. I concluded that I would never hire anyone who played golf. (Don't worry, I no longer have that policy. Some of the most productive people I know love golf and play it religiously.)

So many things in life are wonderful, but they are just not for me. That doesn't mean they aren't right for someone else. It may be in perfect alignment with that person's intention. That is one reason we should never use our own personal values and priorities as the measure by which we judge others.

Of course, there are things all of us should try to eliminate from our lives. There is no healthy amount of arrogance. There is no healthy amount of greed. There is no healthy amount of bitterness. There is no healthy amount of duplicity. There is no healthy amount of unfaithfulness. There is no healthy amount of narcissism. There are certain things you can't keep, even in moderation. They just don't work like that. If you allow even a drop, it will poison every aspect of your soul.

But I also discovered there are other things you cannot have too much of. Contrary to popular belief, you cannot be too kind. You may be too nice, or too compliant, but you can never be too kind. Make a commitment to be extravagant with kindness. Be kind to everyone you meet, in every circumstance, in every condition. I understand that there will be exceptions. After all, none of us is perfect. But when you look back on your life you will want this theme defining who you are: Even when they didn't have to, they showed kindness.

You might as well be extravagant with hope too. No matter what the pessimists will tell you, hope does not detach you from reality. Hope does not blind you to the problems of the world. Hope does not make you shallow. Hope is not denial. I understand that hope gets a bad rap. Hope can easily be confused with delusion, especially when it is used as an escape from reality. It's the person who keeps spending the little money they have to buy lottery tickets, hoping they will win the jackpot. It's the guy who keeps hoping he will lose weight, but never changes his eating habits. It's the woman in an abusive relationship convincing herself that she can change him if she stays. Whenever hope is rooted in luck, or powerlessness, or denial, it is false hope.

But hope can also make you powerful. One of my favorite films of all time is *The Shawshank Redemption*. It's about a man who is imprisoned for a murder he did not commit. In spite of nearly insurmountable odds and the dangers of a brutal and corrupt prison system, he not only survives prison life, he designs an escape plan that eventually sets him free. The most powerful insight in the entire film is when Red says to Andy: "Let me tell you something my friend. Hope is a dangerous thing. Hope can drive a man insane." You cannot break a person who refuses to give up on hope. Hope is the magic behind optimism. Hope reminds you that no matter how bad it gets, you will get through this. If you cannot destroy a person's hope, you cannot destroy them.

If you want to be rare in this world, never give up on hope. Hope is the singular power that can destroy apathy and give you the strength to endure the dark violence of the human story. We cannot escape the reality that this life is full of pain and suffering, violence and injustice, even cruelty and corruption. Yet hope cuts through despair in the same way that light cuts through darkness. Hope makes you contagious. Hope makes you a light.

This one might be harder, but you cannot be too forgiving. Here, if only from a historical perspective, I have to appeal to Jesus, who is the maven of forgiveness. He once told his disciples that they were to forgive their enemies, which didn't go over very well. They asked him how many times would be required to forgive the people who wanted to oppress and destroy them. Jesus' response was "seventy times seven." You can do the math—that's a lot of times. What his disciples understood was that Jesus was not saying you should forgive 490 times, but on the 491st, you can stop forgiving. In his day, seventy times seven was the mathematical equivalent of an infinite number. In other words, Jesus was saying that you cannot forgive too much.

Frankly, I have mixed feelings about this. The idea that I should be forgiven without limits is incredibly appealing to me. The idea that I should forgive *others* without limit is not as palatable. Still, I see the wisdom in it. I've been married for nearly forty years and there is no way we would have made it without forgiveness. So far, so good. I assure you we have tested the limits of forgiveness. It's not the boulders, but the pebbles, that cause a rockslide. It's not the big betrayals that bring down a relationship; it's the countless small things that accumulate into bitterness and resentment. Relationships will only last as long as the forgiveness flows. And that's as true for whole societies as it is for a married couple. There cannot be too much forgiveness in the world. One thing I know for certain is that there will come a time in your life when you'll need forgiveness. Forgiveness will flow freely in your direction if it has always flowed from you to others.

Another thing you cannot have too much of is integrity. This would seem obvious, except I've actually heard people say that you can be too honest for your own good. What they actually mean is that an honest person is dangerous to have in a dishonest organization. I am fascinated by the cultural phenomenon of the "whistleblower." The term itself is an acknowledgment that sometimes there is only one person in a company with the integrity to call out corruption. Sadly, integrity under pressure is such a rare character trait that we've had to come up with a designation for someone who shows it.

The word *integrity* comes from the same etymology as the word *integration*. It means you are undivided. It means that you are the same person in every room, in every circumstance, and in every situation. Integrity means that you are a person of your word, and that is crucial, because trust is the basis of everything good you will ever want to build. Without trust, you cannot have sustained success. Without trust, you cannot have sustained relationships. If you are not trustworthy, everything else that is good about you will collapse in the end. No one will ever accuse you of having too much integrity, so have it in abundance.

There is one more good thing I want to encourage you to indulge in. This one may surprise you, but I sincerely believe that you cannot have too much ambition. Ambition is another quality that's been given a bad rap over the generations. For some reason we've come to believe that the most deeply virtuous people are those who have put to death their ambition. I wish someone had told me earlier in my life, especially in relationship to my spiritual journey, that ambition is both powerful and good. Let me be clear: Ambition is a virtue.

The reason ambition has been seen in such a negative light is that we humans tend to be ambitious about all the wrong things. We have seen too many examples of powerful people whose ambitions were less than virtuous. Take Elizabeth Holmes, for example. She launched her start-up Theranos with claims of having created a blood-testing technology that never existed. Her avarice exceeded her expertise as she raised hundreds of millions of dollars in investments and built a nine-billion-dollar empire. In late 2022 she was sentenced to eleven years in prison for fraud. Even today, as I was writing this chapter, one of my closest friends sent me a link to a news story about an investor he nearly hired to manage his portfolio. It turns out the investor would be indicted for defrauding three banks and numerous investors out of thirty-five million dollars in funds.

Those are only two examples. We could think of any number of people whose ambitions led to their own demise and the destruction of others. But simply because ambition has been misdirected, it doesn't mean that ambition is the problem. It is possible to make ambition a virtue. To become ambitious for the good you are meant to do. To not let those of lesser virtue have greater ambition than you. To live with ambition for the good and the beautiful and the true.

Dictionary.com defines ambition as "an earnest desire for some type of achievement or distinction . . . and the willingness to strive for its attainment." From that description, it's a morally neutral quality. But it's interesting that the site authors go on to use this as the example: "Too much ambition caused him to be disliked by his colleagues."

I believe that we can change the narrative.

"She had so much ambition to do good that she inspired everyone who knew her."

"He had so much ambition to end poverty that not only did he give an immense part of his wealth to alleviate human suffering, he inspired an endless number of others to do the same."

"They had so much ambition, nothing could convince them that they could not make the world better. They would either be a part of the solution, or they would die trying."

The opposite of ambition is apathy. And if ambition has done its fair share of damage throughout human history, it cannot possibly be compared to the damage done by those who have lived apathetic lives. Evil needs the oxygen of apathy to thrive. History is shaped by those who do not believe you can have too much of a good thing. What we need is a revolution of ambition. What the future needs are women and men who are driven to create a better world.

What will you become ambitious for? You cannot have too much freedom. You cannot have too much justice. You cannot have too much compassion. You cannot have too much equality. You cannot treat a person with too much dignity. You cannot love too much. You cannot have too much faith. You cannot have too much hope. These are the virtues that the human spirit needs in abundance.

Make room in your soul for the things that make you a better human. Be ruthless in eliminating everything that is not a reflection of your best self. There is a universe inside you, and like the universe itself, it is ever expanding. You will always have more room to grow. You can explore love all your life and never come to its borders. The same goes for hope and faith and courage and generosity. There will always be more to discover. When you make them a part of who you are, you become limitless. When you pursue the good and the beautiful and the true, it changes you at a fundamental level. It transforms you. You *become* the good and the beautiful and the true.

May the ever-expanding universe inside you become your gift to the world. May everyone who crosses your path be blessed by the person you have become and the world you have created. May you always be a beacon pointing to the noble and honorable and best of humanity. With every breath, may you be a light in dark places, and proof of life to those holding on with a silent desperation. May your life be an inspiration to all the dreamers yet to come.

ACKNOWLEDGMENTS

I would like to express my deepest gratitude to everyone who has played a role in bringing *Mind Shift* to the world.

First and foremost, I want to acknowledge and thank my wife, Kim, who has made forty years of life an adventure and who has been fearless on the journey.

I am also so grateful for my family: Aaron, Mariah, Jake, and Juno for their unwavering support and encouragement. Your love and belief in me inspire me every day, and I could not have done this without you.

I also want to acknowledge my Campodonico family: Steve, Paty, Mia, and Stevie. Thank you for your loving hearts and servant spirits.

To my agent, Esther Fedorkevich, and the Fedd Agency, thank you for your tireless work in advocating for me and this book. Your belief in my writing and vision means the world to me.

I want to thank my editor, Derek Reed, who has worked with me so creatively to refine the manuscript. Your attention to detail and commitment to excellence truly made this book better.

To Tina Constable and the entire publishing team at Convergent, thank you for believing in me and for your commitment to helping me share my message with the world.

I also want to acknowledge my incredible team at Mosaic, who continue to inspire me with their creativity, passion, and dedication to making the world a better place. Your support and encouragement have been a constant source of inspiration and strength. I especially want to thank Cindy Castillo, who has served me and our team with such joy and excellence.

To my friends Jamie and Paulo Lima, Jon Gordon, Edwin Arroyave, Brad and Shanda Damphousse, Ed Mylett, Joel Marion, Lewis Howes, Jacob Koo, Erin Rank, Tiyanjane Dzilankhulani, and Scott Harrison, whose lives have inspired and challenged me to step into this space, thank you for allowing me to share your stories with the world.

I want to thank my McManus Mastermind team: Aaron McManus, Austin St. John, Alisah Duran, Dan Bolton, and Ross Tanner, who bring their unique talents and insights to everything we do. Your commitment to excellence and your willingness to push the boundaries of what is possible have been instrumental.

Finally, thank you to all those who read this book. My hope is that *Mind Shift* will inspire and challenge you to see life through an entirely new lens.

Dream, Risk, Create,

—Erwin Raphael McManus

ABOUT THE AUTHOR

ERWIN RAPHAEL MCMANUS is a mind, life, and cultural architect and an award-winning author and artist. His books have sold over one million copies and have been translated into more than a dozen languages. As a world-renowned communicator, McManus has spoken to millions of people in seventy countries on five continents in stadiums of up to one hundred thousand people. His creative genius has resulted in consulting work with organizations spanning from the NFL to the Pentagon. McManus has spent the last thirty years advising and coaching CEOs, professional athletes, celebrities, billion-dollar companies, universities, and world leaders, and is passionate about helping people destroy their internal limitations and unlock their personal genius. A native of El Salvador, McManus is also recognized internationally for being the founder and lead pastor of Mosaic, a spiritual movement that has inspired millions worldwide. He and his wife, Kim, also lead humanitarian work across the globe. McManus coaches leaders, entrepreneurs, and communicators worldwide through McManus Mastermind as well as through his groundbreaking work on The Seven Frequencies of Communication.

erwinmcmanus.com

ABOUT THE TYPE

This book was set in Garamond, a typeface originally designed by the Parisian type cutter Claude Garamond (c. 1500–61). This version of Garamond was modeled on a 1592 specimen sheet from the Egenolff-Berner foundry, which was produced from types assumed to have been brought to Frankfurt by the punch cutter Jacques Sabon (c. 1520–80).

Claude Garamond's distinguished romans and italics first appeared in *Opera Ciceronis* in 1543–44. The Garamond types are clear, open, and elegant.

SHIFT YOUR MIND

To access free resources and more
content from Erwin Raphael McManus
visit erwinmcmanus.com